"HUNDREDS OF WONDERFUL VACATION POSSIBILITIES. EVELYN KAYE'S BOOK GIVES COUNTLESS DETAILS, AND COMMENTS FROM PEOPLE WHO HAVE TAKEN THE VACATIONS."   *TCE NEWSLETTER, NEW YORK.*

"REST AND RELAX DURING YOUR SUMMER BREAK - FOR FREE. TO FIND OUT HOW, CHECK OUT *FREE VACATIONS*. THIS NEW RELEASE BY EVELYN KAYE GIVES YOU NAMES, ADDRESSSES, PHONE AND FAX NUMBERS, AND COMMENTS OF PEOPLE WHO HAVE TAKEN THE TRIPS."
     LEARNING MAGAZINE: SUCCESSFUL TEACHING TODAY

"AN EXCELLENT RESOURCE GUIDE. A RICH ASSORTMENT OF INFORMATION ON OPPPORTUNITIES AND OFFERS AROUND THE COUNTRY IN NATIONAL PARKS, VOLUNTEER ORGANIZATIONS, HISTORIC PRESERVATION PROJECTS, CAMPGROUND HOSTS, NATURE WALKS, ARCHAEOLOGICAL DIGS. FEATURES FIRST-HAND STORIES FROM TRAVELERS WHO HAVE EXPERIENCED THESE TRIPS."
JACK ADLER, PRODIGY/INTERNET BOOK REVIEWS

"A MONEY-SAVING GUIDE TO HUNDREDS OF RETREATS AND ECOLOGICAL TOURS IN PLACES LIKE ANCIENT ANASAZI SITES IN ARIZONA, NATIONAL PARKS IN CALIFORNIA, CURLEW NATIONAL GRASSLANDS IN IDAHO. EXCURSIONS ARE FREE IF YOU'RE WILLING TO WELCOME VISITORS TO CAMPGROUNDS, LEAD TOURS, AND CLEAR TRAILS." *GOOD TIMES: THE LIFESTYLE MAGAZINE OF MATURE PENNSYLVANIANS*

"TRAVEL AND HAVE EXPERIENCES YOU NEVER DREAMED POSSIBLE. HUNDREDS OF CAREFULLY SELECTED VACATIONS."   *FAMILY TIES MAGAZINE, KANSAS.*

* RECOMMENDED BY *CONSUMER REPORTS TRAVEL LETTER, COUNTRY HOME, SCOUTERS DIGEST, ACTIVE TIMES*, AND OTHER PUBLICATIONS.

"Security is mostly a superstition.
It does not exist in nature, nor do the children of men as a whole
experience it.
Avoiding danger is no safer in the long run than outright
exposure.
Life is either a daring adventure, or nothing.
To keep our faces toward change and behave like free spirits in the
presence of fate is strength undefeatable."

Helen Keller, "Let us Have Faith",1940.

FREE VACATIONS
&
BARGAIN ADVENTURES
IN THE USA

by Evelyn Kaye

A BPP Travel  Resource Guide

FREE VACATIONS & BARGAIN ADVENTURES IN THE USA
by Evelyn Kaye

Published by Blue Penguin Publications
3031 Fifth Street
Boulder, Colorado 80304
Phone: 303-449-8474

Cover design by George Roche Design
Cover photo of Hawaii beach by Reed Glenn

Every effort has been made to ensure the accuracy of the information in this book, but the world of travel changes from day to day. The publisher takes no responsibility for inaccuracies relating to the material included. Readers are urged to contact places listed directly before making travel plans.

This book was designed by Christopher Sarson on Pagemaker® 5.0 for Windows,
using *Garmond* font from Hewlett Packard and *Weissach* Typecase® fonts from Glyphix.

Printed in the United States of America.
First Edition.

ISBN 0-9626231-7-2
Library of Congress No. 95-060400

Books by Evelyn Kaye

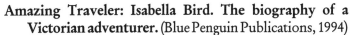

Amazing Traveler: Isabella Bird. The biography of a Victorian adventurer. (Blue Penguin Publications, 1994)

Travel and Learn 1995, 3rd edition (Blue Penguin Publications, 1994; 2nd edition, 1992; 1st edition, 1990) *Awards:* National Mature Media Silver Award, Best Travel Book 1992; Midwest Independent Publishers Association, Award of Merit, Best Travel Book 1993.

Family Travel: Terrific New Ideas for Today's Families (Blue Penguin Publications, 1993). *Award:* Gold First Prize Award for cover and interior design, Colorado Independent Publishers Association, 1994.

Eco-Vacations: Enjoy Yourself and Save the Earth (Blue Penguin Publications, 1991).

College Bound with J. Gardner (College Board, 1988).

The Parents Going-Away Planner with J. Gardner (Dell, 1987).

The Hole In The Sheet (Lyle Stuart, 1987).

Write and Sell Your TV Drama! with A. Loring (ALEK, revised 1993).

Relationships in Marriage and the Family, with Stinnett and Walters (Macmillan, 1984).

Crosscurrents: Children, Families & Religion (Clarkson Potter, 1980).

The Family Guide to Cape Cod with B. Chesler (Barre/Crown, 1979).

How To Treat TV with TLC (Beacon Press, 1979).

The Family Guide to Childrens Television (Pantheon, 1975).

Action for Childrens Television Editor (Avon, 1972).

THE AUTHOR

Evelyn Kaye's travels began when she sailed to Canada from England as a child with her grandmother and ended up living in Toronto for four years. She's traveled ever since looking for as many travel bargains as she can find.

After school in England, she lived for a year in France, and in Israel. She explored Italy, Sicily, Denmark, Sweden, Belgium, the Netherlands, Switzerland, Mexico, Ecuador, Australia, New Zealand, and India.

She's sailed round the Galapagos Islands, camped in an Amazon rainforest, rafted through the Grand Canyon, and horsepacked in Colorado's Sangre de Cristo Mountains. She can find her way around New York City, Chicago, Los Angeles, San Francisco, Denver, Washington DC, and Boston. She recently visited Antarctica to observe icebergs, penguins and seals from a Russian research ship, and Hawaii to explore its hidden beaches.

As a writer and journalist in England, she was the first woman reporter in the *Manchester Guardian*'s newsroom. In the United States, her articles have been published in the *New York Times, Denver Post, McCalls, New York, Travel & Leisure, Glamour, Ladies Home Journal*, and other major publications. She is founder and president of Colorado Independent Publishers Association, a board member of Publishers Marketing Association, past president of the American Society of Journalists and Authors, and a member of the Society of American Travel Writers. She is listed in *Who's Who in America*.

CONTENTS

INTRODUCTION

"There's no cure like travel to help you unravel the worries of living today."
Cole Porter

Free Vacations & Bargain Adventures in the USA will help you find the perfect vacation when you long to get away but don't have a lot of money to spend. Based on my own extensive travels and research, here's an amazing variety of unusual ideas for new and exciting experiences. You'll find in one place the best values available today, with names, addresses, phone and contacts plus descriptions, firsthand comments and prices for hundreds of absolutely free vacations and outstanding bargain adventure trips in North America. This book will save you time, money, and frustration!

Free Vacations was called **Eco-Vacations** in its first edition, and offered dozens of environmental vacation ideas that benefited the earth, many of them absolutely free. This new, completely revised second edition emphasizes free and affordable adventure vacations that are beneficial for the environment—and for you!

Getting Away is Good For You

In today's frenzied world, a vacation is a necessity for your mental health and refreshment of the spirit. When you take off for a month or two, a couple of weeks, one week, or even a weekend in different surroundings, you are exposed to new places, fresh ideas, and a different routine. You have time to see things from a different perspective, and to think about them.

In America, most working people get one or two weeks vacation a year. In many European countries, the benefits of vacations are well-recognized and vacations of three, four, and five weeks are mandated by law or agreement. In Austria, Finland, Luxembourg, Sweden and France, working people get five weeks vacation every year. In the Netherlands, Belgium, Switzerland, Iceland, Italy, Greece, and Belgium, it's four weeks a year.

In the past, those who could afford it used to take off for the summer months and go to the seashore or the country to escape the city's heat. Today in the United States men and women are working longer hours and struggling to keep ahead with far less time for vacations. Even though it may take time and energy to plan a vacation away with family, children, dogs, cats and leaving behind your many commitments, the break is always worth it.

Think about the kind of escape you would enjoy. Does your job keep you sitting all day? An active vacation outdoors where you spend a week in a national forest hiking along trails and clearing the brush will be a revitalizing change. Do you spend your days glued to a computer? Think about taking up a new, active challenge like mountain biking along the trails, or paddling down a river on a rafting trip. Does your work demand intense concentration on details? A real escape would be a laid-back trip to a ranch in Montana, or hiking along open trails in Colorado.

An ideal vacation provides a change of pace from your everyday routine, offers enjoyable new experiences, and gives you time to relax and enjoy what you are doing today, instead of perpetually worrying about tomorrow.

Do vacations cost too much?

As a long-time traveler and travel writer, I am often appalled at the cost of advertised vacations. I blanch at hotel rooms that cost $300 a night—without breakfast. I cringe at luxury resorts that charge a thousand dollars a week for amenities I know are available for less. I hesitate to plunk down my money for a vacation that will empty my savings account when I know I can find the same thing at a better price, if I only look around. I like vacations that give me value for what I spend, without extravagance.

So I've been looking around very carefully for many years to find the best vacation deals. I read reports, I study catalogs, I talk to companies, and I interview travelers. This year, I've put the results of my extensive research and experience into this book, so you can discover how to save money when you take a vacation.

Are there really free vacations?

YES! Many vacations are absolutely free IF you volunteer to help in some way. These opportunities are rarely advertised, but every year, more and more people discover and enjoy them.

You can spend several months, one month, or a few weeks enjoying the Rocky Mountains or the California redwoods or Cape Cod beaches or the lakes of Michigan or the nature reserves of Texas or the bayous of Louisiana or the rivers of Idaho or the forests of New Mexico. While many volunteer openings want you for a month or more, there are others that welcome short-time commitments.

The only money you should have to spend is to get there. My criteria for a free vacation are:

√   Free accommodations, campsite, RV hook-up.

√   Personal expenses of less than $20 a day.

√   Sometimes meals or food stipend provided.

√   Region is interesting vacation area.

√   Activities are fun and not exhausting.

√   Adequate time off.

√   Programs offered by responsible organization.

√   Experienced and knowledgeable leaders.

√   Contact office responds promptly.

√   Recent participants recommend the vacation.

In exchange for your free vacation, you are expected to do specific tasks in a responsible and dedicated manner. Many volunteer positions have dozens of applicants so individuals are carefully chosen based on their abilities and interest. The work is important, and those who hire volunteers want it to be done right.

You'll find that often the best vacations are those in which you participate actively. On a river rafting trip, it's fun to paddle the raft and be part of the team. On a hike, the sense of community is rewarding as you struggle up the hills and slither down the slopes. As a volunteer, you feel a sense of pride and accomplishment as you look at the trail you've cleared or the campground you've supervised or the research project you helped to complete.

Pick Your Preference

Volunteers in state and national parks, national forests or wilderness areas with a sense of willingness, energy and commitment can choose from a range of different jobs. You decide where you'd like to go, and what you'd like to do, and request application forms. Apply early—many popular destinations, such as Alaska and Hawaii, have waiting lists. Take the Quiz in this book to analyze your abilities, and at the end of it you'll find descriptions of what is involved for those who sign up for trail maintenance, or to be campground hosts, interpretive guides, visitor center assistants, backcountry rangers, and more. If you have special skills, you can join research expeditions, or help with computer data, or join wilderness backcountry rangers exploring new regions.

In exchange for your services, you receive benefits depending on the position, the region, and the length of time you stay. Often you get a free campsite or RV site. Sometimes you get free meals, a uniform, or a small stipend to cover your food expenses. Sometimes you get housing, all meals and transportation. Always ask before you go.

In this book you'll find true firsthand experiences from people who have served as volunteers and enjoyed bargain adventure vacations. You can discover exactly what it's like to join a trail crew, serve as a campground host, and plan a bargain adventure for yourself.

Who takes advantage of these vacations?

You'll find people of all ages. Some programs are for high school and college students only, while mature travelers and retirees sign up because it's an economical way to travel and enjoy their free time. One older couple, who spends their winters as campground hosts in Florida, said: "We enjoy the routine at the campground. There's always something interesting to do here. We see families who come back every year. And there's plenty of time to fish."

Why haven't I heard about these vacations before?

Few travel agents tell you about free or inexpensive vacations because they prefer to send you to places where they can earn a commission. So they recommend luxury resorts, major hotel chains, or cruise ships. There's no easy way to find out about free vacations!

These vacations are offered through non-profit groups, such as the American Hiking Society, Rocky Mountain Nature Association, Student Conservation Association, and by the Forest Service, and national and state parks. These groups cannot afford full-page ads in Sunday newspapers or flashy commercials on TV.

That's why I wrote this book—to bring to your attention some of the best vacation bargains still available in the US.

What about an affordable adventure vacation?

There are plenty of small—and large—independent companies that specialize in affordable adventure vacations. Their programs have expanded rapidly in the last ten years. They take you to hike, bike, climb mountains, ski, canoe, raft, run, and more. Often the people who run the companies lead the trip because it's something they love to do. You learn from them and share their enthusiasm for the experience. Some nonprofit groups offer adventure trips, and emphasize environmental concerns along the way.

The bargain adventure companies I've selected for this book have all met the following criteria.

√   Cost is about $100 a day per person, all-inclusive.
√   Programs are led by experienced guides.
√   Good accommodations and meals.
√   Emphasis on nature, preservation, research.
√   Concern with environmental preservation.
√   Places accessible from anywhere in the US.
√   In business for a reasonable length of time.
√   Working address, phone, and fax.
√   Responds to inquiries.
√   Pre-trip orientation where necessary.
√   Provides up-to-date well-designed information materials.
√   Provides names of recent participants.

Free Vacations & Bargain Adventures is a cornucopia of great ideas for outstanding and affordable vacations.

No book is ever written alone. My thanks to the women and men I interviewed about their volunteer and adventure vacations; to the National Park Service, USDA Forest Service and BLM rangers and others out in the wilderness who answered questions and provided up-to-date information.; and to friends who recommended trips they'd taken.

Special thanks to Laura Caruso, an indefatigable copy editor who carefully checked the manuscript at lightning speed; to Linda Castrone for her expert editorial advice; to George Roche for his cover design savvy and patience; to Reed Glenn for taking the time to photograph beautiful beaches; and to my husband, partner, travel companion, and computer whiz Christopher Sarson, who once again transformed a multitude of information into an easy-to-read well-designed travel resource guide.

Browse through the book, make notes of what interests you, and choose a great trip this year!

Happy travels!

Before You Go

How to budget your vacation

Trying to work out if a vacation is worth the price is a difficult game. You have to balance whether you can afford to travel to Alaska and see bears versus how much you really want to spend a week skiing in the mountains. Evaluating the cost of a vacation is something I've learned over the years. I've read thousands of lush, colorful brochures promising me the vacation of my dreams, and leafed through hundreds of beautifully printed catalogs. I know what to look for, how to spot what's included and what's not, and where to find the extremely small print that tells you things you really ought to know but they hope you won't read too carefully.

Research. Before you set out on any trip, spend an evening doing some research. One summer, I planned a rafting trip out West to see part of the country I didn't know. I requested half a dozen brochures from different companies and compared what they offered.

I found that you could travel down a river on a motor powered raft, which was fast but meant you'd hear engines down the canyons. You could join an active trip where you paddled through the rapids as a team member. Or you could choose oar-powered boats with a guide steering the raft while you lazed in the sun. And you could even use an inflatable kayak or paddle boat through the rapids if you wanted a close-up thrill.

One company included the price of a small plane flight to the put-in point. Another paid for hotel accommodations the night before we set out on the trip. Some companies rented tents and sleeping bags while others expected you to bring your own. Some offered gourmet meals prepared by a chef, while others welcomed help with group cooking. Some took you on canyon hikes and nature walks as well as river rafting.

Compare and contrast. I made a list of what was included for comparison. I also thought about the trip itself. Did I want a challenging, exciting adventure or was I in a mood for a more relaxed journey? Should I bring my own equipment and save the rental fees? Was I willing to help make dinner or sit back and let someone else do the cooking? How much difference in cost was there in traveling to the starting point? What part of the country did I want to explore?

I chose a four-day trip down the Yampa River in Colorado. The starting point was a town I could reach by car or bus, so that saved an airfare.

Going Down the Yampa. We put in near Steamboat Springs, and spent four days on the Yampa, an undulating stretch of water that runs through colorful canyons, soaring cliffs, and flat open landscapes. There were paddle or oar-powered rafts, and, for the adventurous, two-person inflatables and kayaks that bounced through the waves. I brought my own tent and sleeping bag, and an air mattress. Our guides were excellent cooks, providing blueberry pancakes for breakfast, buffet salads for lunch, and chocolate cake for dessert.

Summary. The trip delivered everything that I had hoped for when I first began thinking about my vacation. The water was low so the rapids were easy to ride. The group included two sisters, three friends with their two children, and a couple from Missouri on their honeymoon. The guides, friendly, calm, hardworking, were always there to make sure we were enjoying ourselves. There were no hidden extras or unexpected costs. It was the right vacation at the right time and the right price.

Checkpoints

If a vacation price sounds ridiculously low, it may be because nothing is included. Here's what to look for, including the eeensy-tweensy print that is buried somewhere inside.

Airfare. This is a major expense, unless you are awash in Frequent Flyer miles. Is airfare included? Where do you have to fly to in order to join the trip? If the trip starts in Miami and you're in San Francisco, add that to the cost.

Meals. Are all meals provided or are you expected to buy your own meals? This can prove expensive and also time-consuming, if you are in a strange place. Some groups give you vouchers for meals, other provide group meals, and others take you to restaurants to eat out or offer meals at the place you are staying. Make sure you know what is included, and whether you need to budget funds for meals.

Trips and Excursions. Does the price include these? Or will you have to pay separately for each outing or tour? A good company includes the cost in the overall price.

Guides & Leaders. Are these qualified and experienced people? If you are going on a whale-watching tour, is the leader a naturalist or someone who knows about ocean mammals? On a river rafting trip, make sure your guides are qualified and experienced. Don't hesitate to ask about the qualifications of those in charge.

Tips, taxes and additional charges. These are usually mentioned in small print, but always check them out beforehand.

Pre-trip material. Does the company send you helpful information about the trip in advance? It's good to have a detailed itinerary, and a list of what to bring.

Ask questions beforehand. The time to ask about things that worry you or catch your attention is before you set out on your adventure. Before you go, explain that you're allergic to peanut butter or that you get nosebleeds above 3,000 feet or that you snore heavily, and everyone will be happier on your vacation.

VACATIONERS' QUIZ

When you choose an outdoors adventure or volunteer experience, you want to be sure it's for you. The best advice is: Go for it! To help you make your decision, take this personal quiz to determine how you'd fit in.

Hercules or Wimp?

Free vacations can demand strenuous hiking and active outdoors work, or easy walks and time spent meeting people and sitting at a visitor center.

What kind of shape are you in?
    A. Terrific—I run almost every day.
    B. Moderate—I go for walks regularly.
    C. Don't ask—I hate to exercise.

Can you run up the stairs without feeling winded?
    A. You bet!
    B. How many stairs?
    C. No way!

Can you walk a mile with a 30-lb. backpack?
    A. Yes.
    B. I used to do that but...
    C. Never tried!

How do you feel about camping or living in the outdoors?
    A. I just love camping and have done it often.
    B. It's fun as long as it doesn't rain.
    C. I'd prefer a cabin, dorm room, or RV.

How do you cope with high-altitude mountains?
    A. Doesn't affect me!
    B. Get a bit queasy but it wears off.
    C. Never tried it!

Are you affected by damp and cold?
  A. Doesn't affect me!
  B. Yes, I get leg pains and...
  C. Avoid it!
Are you bothered by dust and dirt?
  A. Never notice them!
  B. My sinuses react!
  C. Hate them!

If you answer mostly As, you're ideal for any outdoors volunteer position or adventure vacation. Consider signing up for trail crews, wilderness rangers, and trail maintenance positions. On adventure trips, you'd choose the wildest with the most challenging camping and hiking.

If you have mostly Bs and Cs, you're truthful, and as a volunteer, you'd be happy leading nature hikes, acting as a campground host, giving interpretive presentations, or answering questions at a visitor center. On adventure trips, you enjoy a trip with hikes at an average pace, where you stay in hostels, hotels, or inns, as well as some camping.

Getting Really Personal

How well do you get along with others? Answer the following questions, rating yourself from A to E.

  A - Absolutely!
  B - Better believe it!
  C - Could be me.
  D - Don't have it.
  E - Excuse me?

I welcome new experiences.
I have a sense of adventure.
I have a good sense of humor.
I am usually optimistic.
I have a lot of energy.
I am flexible when plans change.
I am adaptable in different circumstances.
I am usually friendly, and outgoing.
I like meeting new people.
I get along with different people.
I have the ability to cope in a crisis.
I can laugh at myself.

For someone to succeed in a group setting, you should score mostly As, Bs and Cs on this test. Those who organize outdoor and volunteer vacations have found that the kind of people who cope the best are upbeat, optimistic, easygoing and adaptable to unexpected circumstances and different people. However, if you've marked yourself down with a bunch of Ds and Es, and feel a volunteer or adventure vacation is something you want to try, sign up anyway - you'd be a refreshing change from the upbeat optimism of everyone else.

Examine Your Experience

Dozens of activities are available if you want to volunteer or set off on a new adventure. Think about vacations you've enjoyed, and mark the following activities on a scale of:

5 - love doing this.
4 - enjoy this sometimes.
3 - quite like it.
2 - don't care to do it.
1 - never understood how anyone could want to do this.

Answering questions.
Archaeology digs.
Biking.
Canoeing.
Carpentry.
Computers.
Drawing.
Driving a jeep.
Gardening.
Hiking.
History tours.
Kayaking.
Lifesaving.
Machine maintenance.
Mountain climbing.
Photography.
Rafting.
Rowing.
Scuba.
Snorkeling.
Speaking to groups.
Swimming.
Trail clearing.
Video.
Wildlife research.
Writing.

What positions are there?

Take a look at what you checked off. Below is a list of major categories of volunteer positions available. While every volunteer job is different, and the actual work involved varies from place to place, here are brief descriptions of some of the choices for vacations in state and national parks.

Trail Maintenance. Plenty of openings for active, outdoors, energetic individuals. You stay free at a campsite, cabin, RV site or in a nearby community, and sign up for a weekend, a week, two weeks, a month, or longer. Trail crews often welcome short-term volunteers because the work is demanding. You are usually given equipment and training, and there's an experienced leader who directs what's to be done. Those who've worked on trail maintenance enthuse about the camaraderie of a group working together on a specific project, like building a bridge, and the sense of accomplishment when it's done.

Campground Hosts. This is an ideal position for friendly people who are dedicated, responsible, adaptable, able to talk, explain, answer questions, and make people feel welcome. You may be the first person a new camper sees, and you should be able to get along with a variety of personalities. Usually you get a free site for your RV or camper, not a tent. Time commitments are for a month or longer.

Wilderness Rangers. Someone who enjoys demanding hikes, bike rides, or horse-riding will find working in wilderness areas an exciting challenge. You should be self-reliant, experienced in the outdoors, aware of no-impact camping practices, and able to cope with the unexpected. You will check trails, meet hikers, help with surveys, and rely on your own initiative to solve problems. A month or longer is needed for these positions.

Interpretive Guides. If you have a good knowledge of the area and its natural features, biology, geology, and history, and an interest in talking to people about the region, this may be a great position for you. You should be able to lead nature walks and present programs. It's important to enjoy meeting people and explaining the same thing many times. Sometimes you have to stay on the site, but at some places, you can commute from a nearby community.

Visitor Center Assistants. As with campground hosts, you are often the first person to meet visitors and campers. You should be able to answer questions and provide information, talk to people, deal with different personalities, and cope with emergencies. In some places, you sell books and other items. You live in an RV, cabin, dormitory, or provided housing, or may commute from a nearby community.

Researchers. If you are skilled in a particular field of natural history, environmental science, computer technology, or marine biology, you can assist on research projects. These range from counting birds and watching bears to testing water samples and observing vegetation growth.

Archaeologists. There are many places where ancient artifacts and historic sites are discovered, examined, and restored. These range from pre-historic digs to rebuilding old fire towers. If you like investigating the past, you will find plenty of openings. You can even assist paleontologists looking for dinosaur bones.

Actors and musicians. Historic parks look for creative individuals to tell the story of the past in an entertaining way. If you have performing skills, there are several openings, and your talent will be appreciated.

Photographers and artists. The history and development of specific sites and buildings is carefully documented with drawings and photographs. Some sites have a darkroom, and others provide materials. If you have skills in these areas, you will be welcome as an assistant.

Writers, graphic designers, and computer experts. The parks need help in creating publications, newsletters, trail materials, maps, lists, and information that visitors and others often request. Assistance is also needed from people who can input computer data, help with library catalogs, file, organize schedules, and keep track of research data.

Carpenters and masons. Experienced construction workers are always welcome, to rebuild historic structures, fix what is falling down, and maintain park buildings.

And now...

You have analyzed your skills, decided your preferences, and examined how you are best suited as a volunteer. Look through the book at the FREE volunteer openings. You will be able to judge those opportunities where your personality and aptitude fits exactly with the requirements, and then contact the correct office for application forms and information.

One final note:

National park volunteers must complete official application forms, reprinted in the appendix at the end, with descriptions of past work and study experience as well as personal references. Popular parks and specialized positions often have many applicants. For the best chance at getting what you want, apply early.

STORIES FROM THE FIELD

What's it really like to go off on a volunteer vacation, serve as a campground host, take off on a bargain adventure trip? Is it only for people in tiptop condition? Will it turn out to be absolutely exhausting, so that you'll need a vacation to recover? What will the food be like? How about the other people? Will you feel out of place if you haven't done this before? Is it any fun?

The best people to ask are those who've tried volunteer and bargain vacations recently and who are happy to share with you what happened to them. Here are stories from an English high school student and an older hiker about clearing trails, from a retired couple who spend their summers as volunteers looking after a lighthouse, and from my own experiences of adventure vacations.

Working on a Trail Crew

A Student's View
by Larissa Howard

Larissa Howard is a high school senior from England who came over with a friend to help build part of the Colorado Trail near Breckenridge, Colorado.

Colorado Trail Crew #13 first met on August 13th, all pretty well ready for a week that promised to hold a lot of experiences, not the least of which was WORK. However, work was only going to take up a small portion of our time together; the rest seemed to be wide open for possibilities.

One of the first things that struck me was the diversity of the people, especially as my friend and I had come from England. Seeing so many distant areas of America represented meant we were really going to get to know some of the country's people. In fact Steve's drive from Pennsylvania took longer than our flight from London.

So with these people of different ages from different places, the working day included more than just work. The beauty of the scenery that made up our raw materials also suggested not much could go wrong. Trail work was part of the day's schedule, and we built 4,985 feet (Steve won the pool with the closest guess).

What with all that work, digging up those hardy roots and rocks, camping and cooking in tents, braving whatever the Colorado weather might throw, it could be deduced that the end result was a hardy bunch of strong, fit and indestructible workers. Things did not quite work out like that! The presence of the Breckenridge Recreation Center, three miles

"It has to be said that looking at a line of trail stretching before you, that you built, is immensely satisfying; it feels worthwhile."
Larissa Howard

away, complete with swimming pools, whirlpools, hot tubs, and steaming showers did rather destroy the "roughing it" experience. Evidence of the comparative ease of our lifestyle can be found in the compulsive actions of some - jogging, reading, and teeth cleaning. The food was pretty good, too.

It was not only the strange habits of certain people that provided amusement, there was a humorous blooming romance that ran the whole week. The progression of affection was impressive—whispered invitations to lunch and square dancing—culminating in Juliet's last lunch when Romeo carried a cold beer up the mountain and carved out a table for two in the dirt. Unfortunately, Juliet took an early departure on Thursday and Romeo's withdrawal symptoms showed.

This is not to suggest that the week was only composed of lighthearted fun and games. Quite apart from all the heavy work, our two rest days proved more taxing than relaxing. Sunday we took a Gestapo-style march up to Georgia Pass and back, with finally successful attempts to climb Mt. Quandary (14,165 feet) in hailstones, rain, lightning, and forceful winds.

Basically, the week had it all. Everyone owes a huge debt to Gene Cash, our highly effective yet amazingly relaxed (if a little bit clean-gloved) leader, and his words of wisdom: "Never let the goal compromise your good judgment."

A Hiker's View
by Richard Nolde

Richard Nolde from Connecticut planned a week of trail work and then a hike along the Colorado Trail as his vacation. He worked on a section of the trail at an elevation of 10,600 feet, and stayed at a campsite 1.5 miles below Kennebec Pass.

The Colorado Trail represents more than just a physical pathway for me; it is the epitome of what volunteer activism can achieve. The people I have met during this week on the trail crew impress me mightily. It is the dedication and spirit of these volunteers that will bring me back again and again, which is not to suggest that there is anything wrong with the scenery either.

Our crew includes people of all ages with quite a variety of backgrounds. The younger end of the spectrum is represented by five students from Europe. The other end of the spectrum is represented by a number of retired couples, with highest seniority held by Hobie, now 72, who returned to hiking last year after heart bypass surgery.

Everyone works according to his or her own ability and desire, but one thing has become very clear; age is not the determining factor with regard to the pace at which individuals work. Few of us can keep up with the veterans of other trail crews, but it does not matter. We work together in a way that is rare in the environments in which I spend most of my time.

There are several major-league climbers and distance hikers in the crew. Other members appear to be somewhat less extreme in the pursuit of their recreational goals but equally dedicated to the Colorado Trail and all are essential to the task at hand. Our culinary director and lunch supplies manager keep the lot of us going all week long. And of course how could we hope to accomplish anything without Tom's dedication to keeping the coffee flowing!

For newcomers like myself, the trail building standards set by the Heckmans, a father and sons team that comes back year after year, were an inspiration in themselves. Sean and I seem to share the honors for resident computer nerds, but we manage to get through most of the week without descending to geek talk, and even then we focus on a program I am writing that might be of use to hikers.

These crews have become a family affair for several groups. Larry is here with his sister and brother-in-law. Larry's wife Dawn will join us on Friday and rumor has it that she will bring some excellent homemade cookies. Merle's wife, Uta, and daughter Anne are on this crew, and of course there is Max, the wonder dog, now a bit too arthritic to make the daily climb to the worksite, but very much a part of the effort in spirit at least.

After dinner in the evenings, there is time for conversation, poetry, and music. Patty has brought a guitar, and there are several players amongst us. With a little effort we manage to keep the instrument in tune in spite of the rapidly changing evening temperatures. The fare ranges from popular songs known mostly by the students to old standards better known by the seniors.

I am completely taken off guard when Tom recites the soliloquy from Shakespeare's *Henry V* that takes place before the battle of Harfleur. Equally intriguing but completely different are poems by Robert Service, *The Shooting of Dangerous Dan McGrew,* and *The Cremation of Sam McGee.* Lewis Carroll's *Jabberwocky* and an assortment of other short works fill out the poetry department.

Due to the high fire hazard in the forest, we cannot have a campfire. Instead, we cluster under the tarps or sit on logs at the edge of the clearing by the forest service cook tents until weary bones and the evening chill drive us to our sleeping bags or campers. Given that breakfast call is 6:00 am, most of us turned in early, and some nights the crowd is already thinning out by 8:30.

On the last day, when breakfast is over, the group will soon be dispersing to all corners of the country, from Washington State to Texas to Connecticut, to say nothing of the foreign students who will return to Europe after a second week of trail crew duty. The forest service camp is pretty much dismantled, and the equipment loaded by 7:30 am, and people are beginning to leave to catch flights or start their long drives. After a memorable week of work, I am ready to take off on my week's hike.

(Reprinted by permission of the Colorado Trail Foundation)

What to bring on a trail clearing trip

Tent or sleeping system with rain fly, ground cloth, closed-cell foam pad or insulated air mattress, and sleeping bag good to 25 degrees F.

Work clothing: long pants, work gloves, sturdy work or hiking boots.

Warm clothing: hat, gloves, sweater, long underwear, long sleeve shirt or sweatshirt, warm jacket, and wool socks. Overnight temperatures may be cold.

Rain gear: waterproof jacket and rain pants.

Backpack to carry all your equipment.

Day pack for lunch, jacket, and rain gear.

Eating utensils: cup, plate, fork, knife and spoon.

Flashlight and extra batteries.

Sun protection: sunscreen, lip balm, hat with brim.

Toilet articles: tooth brush, soap, towel.

Eye protection: sun glasses or safety glasses for flying rock chips.

Mosquito repellant.

First Aid items: aspirin, mole skin, bandage, antiseptic, skin cream.

Water bottles: Two one-quart bottles are recommended.

Volunteer Vacation in a Lighthouse

Gene and Lennie Wilkins are retired physical therapists, both 67, and their home is in Texas. A few years ago they decided to look into volunteer vacations in state and national parks. They asked their local library for addresses, and wrote off to several places for information. Most replied quickly.

After studying the material, Gene and Lennie chose Apostle Island National Lakeshore in northern Wisconsin, a scenic archipelago of 22 islands and 2,500 acres of peninsula in Lake Superior. They sent off their detailed application forms in the winter, knowing that decisions are made in early spring. Soon they heard they had been accepted, and this year will be their third year of volunteering in Wisconsin.

"The economics are the great attraction - we couldn't go to any place as beautiful as this and stay for three months and be able to afford it," says Gene. "Our friends are envious, and we just love going there. We bring our RV and they provide free hook-ups and everything else at the site, and it costs us less to stay there than to live in Texas. The first year we arrived in shorts and T-shirts in May - and nearly froze. It doesn't warm up at the lake until July."

Lennie says: "We go for the summer, from June to Labor Day. The weather is cool - it's so refreshing - and I love the lakes and the scenery. There are mosquitoes and black flies, but they come and go."

The park provides volunteers with shirts, patches, jackets, nametag and a cap, and a stipend to cover some travel costs. There's also a three-day orientation program at the beginning of the summer, when they travel by boat to see all the islands.

Lennie spends her days at the Visitor Center on the

Dear Tess,

I hope you get to be a national park volunteer when you grow up. Your grandmother and I are volunteering during the summer here at Apostle Islands National Lakeshore. Shortly after Christmas last year, we sent inquiries to the volunteer coordinators at a number of national parks. We got addresses from our local library. We sent inquiries regarding their needs for volunteers so early because the coordinators like to have time to review applicants, make assignments and prepare schedules by early spring. Nearly all of the coordinators answered our letters, most sent applications, and some even called for further information. We chose the Apostle Islands National Lakeshore. They accepted our application and by mid-spring we knew we were coming to the Apostle Islands.

We've been having fun working and working having fun. I have been able to be a caretaker of a magnificent 112-year-old lighthouse on an island, and a relief campground host on a different part of the same island. Grandmother has supported the park staff at a visitor center issuing camping permits and telling visitors about the activities and the areas of interest around the lakeshore. I didn't know that she was so smart.

Tess, you would enjoy the beautiful forests and animals and birds here. We have seen eagles, bears, and I don't know how many beautiful wildflowers. The lakeshore beaches, rocky shores, and sea caves are spectacular, and the tours of the lighthouse will be unforgettable.

We particularly like the opportunity we have had to associate with an extraordinary variety of great people who enjoy working in or visiting the outdoors. The park rangers are truly professional and skillful in meeting their considerable responsibilities in preserving the park for all of us, and granddaughters like you. We also have met many other volunteers of all ages and backgrounds who help the rangers protect the park and provide services to visitors. There are school teachers, college students, computer programmers, and many others, young and older. Park rangers have said that if we volunteers were not here to provide backup support for them, many park activities or visits to the historic sites would have to be reduced or discontinued.

The park has provided us not only much time to visit the surrounding country, but a campsite for our RV, a chance to learn from nature and history, and, of course, unlimited opportunities to meet people from the whole world in an unbelievable outdoor and historic setting.

As you grow up we intend to bore you mightily with stories of the summer we spent in the Apostle Islands. So say your prayers tonight and give a special thanks to your country and the National Park Service.

Granddad and Grandmother

mainland, at Little Sand Island. "I issue camping permits, provide information about the islands and cruise services, sell brochures, and do some bookkeeping. I love it - it feels like fun, not like work, though I'm there all day, for five days a week, and sometimes six."

Gene loves lighthouses. "The allure of Apostle Islands was the fact there were several lighthouses. Sand Island lighthouse was built in 1881, and the others were built at different times. The coastguard is responsible for the lights, and the park service looks after the historic buildings. We volunteers keep them open and provide access to them for the visitors who come. Otherwise they'd have to close them up. We give tours, and explain the history, and show people around."

The primary lighthouse keeper has 10 days or two weeks living in the lighthouse, and then four days or a week off. Gene takes over when they take off. Though the building has no running water or electricity, there is a propane fridge, stove, and heater, some solar-powered lights, and an outhouse. Gene looks after the grounds, does light housekeeping, conducts tours for visitors, and enjoys the views. All drinking water and food are brought from the mainland, though the lake water can be used for washing.

What's it's like alone on an island lighthouse? "Fantastic! Not at all scary," asserts Gene. The living quarters are spacious and comfortable - the lighthouses were designed for a keeper, an assistant, and their families, so there are bedrooms, sitting rooms, kitchen, den, and more.

"What I love about the island is the solitude," said Gene. "The tour boats only come over three times a week from the mainland. The rest of the time sea kayakers, sailboats and power boats drop in every now and then. Also, the kind of person who visits the Apostle Islands really wants to see them because they're not easy to reach, so you find people interested in preserving and looking after what is here."

When he's not at the lighthouse, Gene volunteers as a campground host, or goes back to the mainland.

"When you stay at a place for a few months, you are more than a visitor on vacation for a week or two. You become part of a community, and learn about it, and that's what makes it worthwhile," he said.

(Reprinted by permission of Around the Archipelago newsletter.)

Code of Responsibility for Volunteers

BE SURE.

Look into your heart and know that you really want to help other people.

BE CONVINCED.

Do not offer your services unless you believe in the value of what you are doing.

ACCEPT THE RULES.

Don't criticize what you don't understand. There may be a good reason: find out why.

SPEAK UP.

Ask about things you don't understand. Don't coddle your doubts and frustrations until they drive you away or turn you into a problem worker.

BE WILLING TO LEARN.

Training is essential to any job well done.

WELCOME SUPERVISION.

You will do a better job and enjoy it more if you are doing what is expected of you.

BE DEPENDABLE.

Your work is your bond. Do what you have agreed to do. Don't make promises you can't keep.

BE A TEAM PLAYER.

Find a place for yourself on the team. The lone operator is pretty much out of place in today's complex community.

(from USDA Forest Service, Colorado)

Affordable Hawaii Escape

When you love to travel, you learn how to save money. If you don't, you have to quit traveling. People who rarely travel are always amazed at friends who jet off to Sweden and Senegal and South America, and still manage to eat and pay the rent. I'm going to share with you the nitty-gritty secrets of how you can plan bargain vacations.

It's not difficult but it does take time BEFORE you leave. Are you someone who throws everything into a bag, rushes off to the airport and doesn't give your vacation a moment's thought until you arrive? To save money, you have to change your ways. Spontaneous last-minute travel sounds easy, but it's always the most expensive and least satisfying. Booking an airplane ticket two days ahead of time means you pay the highest rates. Calling a hotel when you get off the plane jet-lagged and frazzled means you'll take the first available room, and not have time or energy to look for the better places. Yes, travel agents can give you some advice. But they are not interested in real bargains—those you have to discover for yourself. Spend a few hours at least three months before you leave to research your options, and you can cut your vacations costs substantially.

Before we took our vacation in Hawaii, we spent time doing research, planning, comparing prices and booking ahead of time so that we could really enjoy a wonderful week of soft sandy beaches, three meals a day, comfortable places to stay, interesting sightseeing, a couple of easy hikes, and time to read and relax. Our total for eight days was $880.00 including room, meals, entertainment and the odds and ends you spend along the way. Just for comparison, the cost of a room—no breakfast, no meals—at a first-class hotel in Hawaii

HAWAII TOURIST BUREAU

2270 Kalakaua Avenue, Suite 801
Honolulu HI 96815
Phone: 808-923-1811 or 415-392-8173

HOSTELLING INTERNATIONAL

733 15th Street NW, #840
Washington, DC 20005
Phone: 800-444-6111

BED & BREAKFAST OFFICES
B&B Honolulu

3242 Kaohinani Drive
Honolulu HI 96817.
Phone: 800-288-4666

B&B Hawaii

PO Box 449, Kapaa, HI 96746
Phone: 800-733-1632

CAMPING
City and County Campgrounds

Dept. of Parks & Recreation
650 S. King Street, Honolulu
Phone: 808-523-4525

State Campgrounds

Division of Parks
1151 Punchbowl Street, Room 310,
Honolulu, HI 96813.
Phone: 808-587-0300

runs from about $200 a night to $500 and more.

How did we do it? I'm going to take you through the process, step by step, and you can discover the secrets and techniques for all your bargain vacations. We had visited Hawaii before, so we knew what to expect and what we liked doing. On adventure camping trips with a group we'd visited different islands. We'd also traveled around on our own, staying in hotels and B&Bs.

Preparation Schedule
Three months before D-Day (Departure Day)

Our D-Day was January so we started planning in October. First, we checked out airline prices. After New Year's Day and the holiday season, prices from Colorado to Honolulu are sometimes lower. We chose to use our frequent flyer miles and January 9 was the date offered closest to the time we could take off from work.

Next, off to the library and bookstore. There are dozens of guides to Hawaii, and this time I used Frommer and Lonely Planet guides, Ray Riegert's *Hidden Hawaii*, and Craig Chisholm's *Hawaiian Hiking Trails*. It's also fun to check recent travel magazines for articles on Hawaii—*Travel & Leisure, Conde Nast Traveler, Travel/Holiday*. The computer literate can use travel forums on the Internet and other services.

First call was to the Hawaii Tourist Bureau, which provided a booklet of accommodations, camping information, and a map. Inexpensive places to stay included Hostelling International, listed in this book. Two Bed and Breakfast Services cover all of Hawaii. B&B Honolulu is the larger service with 489 units, while B&B Hawaii has only 34.

Camping is easy anywhere in Hawaii because it rarely gets cold, though you should expect rainshowers. Permits are required from different offices, and you have to apply in person for city and county campgrounds. There's no camping in Oahu's city parks on Wednesday or Thursday nights. State campgrounds have a five-day stay limit.

Two months before D-Day.

We'd collected enough information, and we were ready to make some decisions. When you travel with companions, it's important to express what you want from a vacation and to listen to what they expect. Now is the time to say "My dream is to sleep on the beach every day" and your partner to explain "I want to climb the highest mountain there." This is followed by discussion, sometimes animated and emotional.

After we talked, we concluded we'd like to spend time on the beach and outdoors, eat at restaurants, not cook for

WAIKIKI BARGAIN HOTELS
The Breakers
 Phone: 800-426-0494
The Hawaiiana
 Phone: 800-367-5122

DON'S PLACE
 Ali'i Bluffs Windward B&B
 46-251 Ikiiki St., Kaneohe, HI 96744
 Phone: 800-235-1151

ourselves, take a couple of easy hikes, and spend a day or two sightseeing in Honolulu. We also agreed not to bring things related to home or work: he agreed to leave his laptop computer at home, and I didn't lug my riding boots along. We made the following decisions.

√   We'd stay on one island, Oahu, and explore it, instead of flying off to two or three.

√   We would not stay in a hostel.

√   We would not go camping.

√   We'd try and find a bargain hotel in Waikiki Beach.

√   If that didn't work out, we'd try B&Bs.

√   If necessary, we could stay outside the Honolulu area.

√   We would rent a car.

One month before D-Day.

We began calling places to stay. The first setback was that the two bargain hotels near Waikiki Beach were booked up. Other hotels were too expensive.

B&Bs were the next choice, a chance to stay with residents. I'm someone who usually avoids cheery chats at breakfast; please talk to me later in the day. Over the years staying in B&Bs, I've learned that the good outweighs the disasters. You meet the locals, learn what it's like to live in a vacation area, get good advice, and stay in interesting places. Once we arrived to find that the bed wasn't made, the hostess had gone to a party, and the room didn't have any lights. Once our hosts wouldn't stop talking so we could hardly get out of the house. But most times, it's been excellent.

We called the B&B services as well as a couple of places in guidebooks and from the Tourist Bureau's Accommodations booklet. Don's place sounded like just what we wanted. On the windward side of the island, in Kanoehe, quiet, off the main road, our own room and bath, breakfast served by the pool, and $75 a night. But Don had only three days available. The other Hawaii B&B Services said they could find us somewhere for the last five days. We should call when we arrived.

After checking car rental prices, we booked the cheapest one we could pick up at the airport.

Two weeks before D-Day.

We had a car, we had somewhere to stay, we had an outline of what we wanted to do. Now we checked what we needed to take. I invested in a new swimsuit. My husband dusted off the fancy pair of thong sandals he'd been given as a present. We planned to pack one carry-on bag each and a daypack for on-the-way essentials as well as for hikes and beach outings.

THE NEAREST BEACH
Kailua Beach Park
N. Kalaheo Avenue, Kailua

HARRY'S CAFE
629 Kailua Road, Kailua
Phone: 808-261-2120

D-Day

We faxed our itinerary to our two grown children. In the early morning dark of a Colorado winter, we drove to the airport to fly to Hawaii.

So did it all work out? Well, here's the journal of what we did, and how we spent our time and money.

Hawaiian Journal

Day 1. Arrive and adjust. Hawaii is 2,000-plus miles from San Francisco, and three hours ahead of Mountain Time. It's best to pretend you're on Hawaiian time, stay up as long as you can and go to bed when everyone else does. We arrived in the early evening after a long day of traveling from Colorado, and had a long wait for the car. We drove to the bed-and-breakfast in Kaneohe. It was charming private house filled with Victorian furniture, paintings and a view of the ocean. Every corner of our cozy room had a doll or bowl or antique artifact.

After unpacking, we asked directions to the nearest beach, a few miles away and a hotspot for windsurfers during the day. We parked, took off our shoes, and set off barefoot on the cool sands to watch the sliver of new moon rise higher in the soft dark sky. The waves were lapping at the shore and the stars shone like newly polished diamonds in the warm air and the palm tree leaves rustled loudly above us. A fisherman said "Aloha" as we walked by, and the noise and rush of the long day's traveling seemed to evaporate completely.

We stopped in at Harry's Cafe for dessert—hot chocolate and delicious cheesecake—and had no trouble falling asleep when it was time to go to bed.

Day 2. Fresh papaya, toast, cereal, tea, coffee, and whatever you want was waiting at a table by the pool for breakfast. The pool turned out to be square and very deep, designed for dedicated divers, not desultory swimmers. Don, our host, was friendly, helpful, and ready to give advice on where to go.

We were determined to go to a beach but avoid TTT. That's the Tourist Tan Tragedy, when you stay out in the sun all day because it feels SOOO good and then get sunburnt SOOO badly you can't move for days. I've done it, and I've learned. We took sunscreen, long-sleeved shirts, a bottle of water, and sun hats, and set off along Route 83 to find a peaceful beach.

The views around every corner took my breath away - it was like driving through a Hollywood movie. The only difficulty was trying to decide which beach was more perfect when at every bend in the road I could see a vista of turquoise sea, foam-tipped waves, palm trees, and sun-warmed clean

THE PERFECT SPOT
Malaekhana State Recreation Area
Kamehameha Highway, Laie

KUALOA RANCH
PO Box 650, Ka'a'awa, HI 96730
Phone: 808-237-7321

A WONDERFUL RESTAURANT
Ahi Kahuku Restaurant
Kamehameha Highwa, Kahuku, HI
Phone: 808-293-5650

white sand. We stopped at Kualoa Beach Park, marked by Molokii Island or Chinaman's Hat offshore, with a park and curving beach.

Along Route 83 we discovered *the* perfect spot about 23 miles north of Kaneohe: Malaekhana State Recreation Area. A stroll under the palm trees in the park leads to a soft sandy beach that curves round a perfect bay that is absolutely deserted. Distant waves crash against the outer reef and rocks to roll gently on to the shore. We spent most of the morning walking, reading, paddling, and dozing, moving from sun to shade under the trees. At low tide, five people waded through the waves to Goat Island a few hundred yards offshore, where there's a bird refuge, coral beach and camping facilities.

We had a picnic lunch, buying sandwiches from a stand, and stopped on the way back at Kahana Valley State Park about 14 miles north of Kaneohe where the road turns sharply inland and curves round the bay. The sun was sinking behind us. We sat on the beach as the lengthening shadows of the trees slowly spread across the sand. The water was shallow and rippling with waves breaking much farther out. It was peaceful and still.

Day 3. From Kualoa Beach Park, we turned off to visit Kualoa Ranch. Set on 4,000 acres overlooking the ocean, it's a working horse ranch. There were a couple of men practicing roping in the arena, two women riding round the big field, and dozens of horses eating in the corral. You can book one- or two-hour horseback or mountain bike trail rides, or sign up for a day-long expedition with a boat ride to an island picnic, beach games, and a catamaran ride into the bay for snorkeling.

Driving up the highway looking for a lunch place, we discovered a wonderful restaurant on the right-hand side about a mile after the Kahuku Sugar Mill, set back from the road. It's a local restaurant built in the 1900s, famous for its fabulously fresh shrimp, sunfish and clams. When it's too hot to sit outside at picnic tables, enjoy the indoors with cushioned wicker chairs, ceiling fan whirling slowly, and the view through the window of palm trees waving against the blue sky. We sat inside and had a wonderful plate of shrimp, with cold drinks and ice cream to finish.

After lunch we drove to Sunset Beach on Route 83. Here's where the real surfers hang out and try their skills on major waves as well as the nearby Banzai Pipeline. A surfing competition was underway. About a hundred people sat on the beach, staring at the waves, or peering through binoculars. A loudspeaker could hardly be heard above the thunder of crashing surf. I could see small black figures on surf boards

KAY'S VACATION RENTAL
232 Awakea Road, Kailua, HI 96734
Phone: 808-261-5174

WINDWARD POI BOWL
Windward Plaza
Kamemeha Highway, Kaneohe

suddenly appear, balance perilously for a few moments just below the tops of giant curling waves and disappear in a mountain of foam. Then a head would surface in the calm water between the waves, and you saw a figure swimming frantically out to sea to avoid the crash of the next wave.

Day 4. Today we moved to our next B&B, Kay's Vacation Rental. On a quiet suburban street only a few blocks from Kailua Beach Park, our new home had a private entrance into a converted garage which offered a large sunny room with bed, living room area with TV, fully equipped kitchen, and bathroom. Our hosts were a New Zealand couple and their two children who gave us the keys and told us where everything was. A friendly gecko lived behind the curtains and ate any visiting insects.

We planned a hike to Waimea Falls and drove up to Waimea Falls Park. It was disappointing to find a commercial park—no free hiking—and entrance fees of $19.95 per adult - way above our hiking budget. Busloads of tourists arrived for organized trolleycar tours along paved roads. Later, we took a guided nature walk to Waimea Falls at a reduced rate, in pouring rain! We found manicured displays of carefully marked plants, trees, and flowers, recreations of traditional Hawaiian homes, and a Disney-like park designed for large groups.

We consulted our hiking guidebook, and decided the Hauula Loop Trail, classified as an easy 2.5-mile loop, sounded about our level. The trailhead is just off Highway 83 down a road near Hauula Beach Park with a parking area. A wide path climbs steadily under pines and guava trees, with inspiring views over the green fields and farms of Hauula and the Pacific Ocean. The air was cloudy and cool, a refreshing change after the burning sun, and it was peaceful, lush and green under the trees, quite different from the beach.

That evening, as we drove back on King Kamehameha Highway, we noticed a Hawaiian restaurant at the end of a row of stores in a shopping plaza. It was a small friendly place, with half a dozen tables and a menu chalked up on a board. So we had dinner at Windward Poi Bowl. Served simply on paper plates and with plastic utensils, the genuine Hawaiian menu provides a variety of dishes, all steamed, well-cooked and tasty. Try pork wrapped in taro leaves, rice, poi, salmon salad with onion sauce, pieces of beef cooked so they taste like soft beef jerky or chicken. On a weekday evening around 7 pm, we were the only customers, though apparently it's busier on weekends. The meal was delicious and inexpensive.

Dessert was ice cream from Baskin-Robbins at the Kailua Shopping Center, and we strolled next door to explore the

HONOLULU BOOKSHOP
Kailua Shopping Center
590 Kailua Road, Kailua, HI
Phone: 808-261-1996

MARITIME MUSEUM
Pier 7
Honolulu Harbor
Phone: 808-536-6373

ALA MOANA BEACH PARK
Ala Moana Beach Drive, Honolulu

IOLANI PALACE
South King Street, Honolulu
Phone: 808-522-0832

Honolulu Bookshop, which has a superb and extensive collection of books about Hawaiian culture and history, and some magnificent photography books, too.

Day 5. For sightseeing in Honolulu, we started with the new Maritime Museum on Pier 7, right on the waterfront. The audiotape guide, narrated by the late William Conrad, is included in the price of admission, and explains Hawaiian maritime history from the Polynesians to the present.

The main room is dominated by two life-size models of huge, smooth, koa wood skiffs. Around the walls and in display cases are photographs and relics of oars, carved ivory scrimshaw made by sailors on whaling ships, harpoons, fishing lures, knives and ropes. There's a video of a real whaler harpooning a whale from an old silent movie, details of the amazing voyage of a 1990s Polynesian canoe that went from Honolulu to New Zealand using traditional navigation techniques, a recreation of a cruise ship, a selection of jazzy surfboards, and photographs of yacht racing.

The Falls of Clyde, moored next to the Museum, is the last four-masted schooner in existence. It's in the process of restoration, and you can walk aboard to see the refurbished captain's quarters with gleaming wood and brass, and the kitchen area below.

The Aloha Tower Center is next door at Pier 9, a Hawaiian version of a waterfront plaza, similar to Boston's Faneuil Hall and New York's South Street Seaport.

For lunch, we picked the Steakhouse on the second level because it had a great view from its big windows. The menu had sandwiches, salads, and fish as well as steak. At other tables men in suits and women with briefcases and notebooks were taking business lunches. Families ordered pink drinks with little umbrellas so their children could play with them. An older couple had brought their granddaughter on a special visit, and two women at a nearby table chatted with them. Outside the sun dazzled down on the blue ocean, a huge liner slowly eased along the waterway, and planes droned overhead coming in to land at Honolulu Airport.

No day in Hawaii is complete without a beach break. Try Ala Moana Beach Park. It's a popular place for city residents. Its calm shallow waters in a sheltered bay are ideal for children to play, swimmers to do laps, and beginners to snorkel. We spent a pleasant afternoon on the sands, and watched the sun set dramatically behind a bank of purple clouds.

Day 6. A visit to Old Honolulu took us to the Royal Iolani Palace which is sometimes open for tours. However, the day we arrived, it was draped in black by Hawaiian

MISSION HOUSES MUSEUM
South King Street, Honolulu
Phone: 808-531-0481

BISHOP MUSEUM
1525 Bernice Street, Honolulu
Phone: 808-847-3511

SAENG'S THAI CUISINE
315, Hahani Street, Kailua
Phone: 808-262-9727

royalists to mark the 1894 trial and imprisonment of Hawaii's last queen, Liliokulani. Directly across the street is a striking statue of King Kamehameha, a glistening gilded figure in a ceremonial robe, the first king to unite Hawaii's islands and tribes into a nation. We were fortunate to be able to attend a performance at the Judiciary Center with many native Hawaiians in the audience. Actors presented a dramatized re-enactment of the US military trial of the Queen to commemorate her imprisonment.

Across the street is Kawaihao Church, built in 1842 of coral blocks. In the cemetery are historic tombstones of some of Hawaii's earliest residents. Opposite is the Mission Houses Museum which offers a tour of the New England homes that were brought here in 1821 to house missionary families.

Continuing our historic mood, we went to the Bishop Museum, housed in a 19th-century building. The day we arrived there was a presentation by women in traditional costumes singing, chanting, and dancing. The Museum often has special events as well as demonstrations of Hawaiian crafts. The original building and the new additions offer an eclectic display of old Hawaiian artifacts including the dazzling feather capes worn by royalty, harpoons from whalers, and vintage photographs. There is also an excellent bookstore.

Day 7. You can find an untouched piece of Hawaii on the leeward side of Oahu. Few people visit and the guidebooks hardly mention it. You follow the Farrington Highway west as it winds past the airport along the shore to Paradise Cove, and continue on to the Ilhani, a new luxury resort, set on a sheltered lagoon with a soft arc of sand. There are four beautiful lagoons with sandy beaches, all open to the public. Just say "I'm going to the beach" to the hotel's security guards if they ask.

Farther along the shore, the beaches are sometimes windy and wild, and often rocky, not sandy. The Waianae Mountains loom on the mountain side, edging the road. You see small Hawaiian communities, gas stations, windswept beach parks, and spectacular surfing on the waves. The road ends at a military center.

For the last evening, we chose a celebration dinner at a recommended Thai restaurant, where the family at the next table had month-old twins sleeping peacefully in their baby seats as the family celebrated their mother's birthday.

Day 8. Time for a last stroll along Kailua Beach Park to watch the red and gold and purple windsurfer sails dotting the choppy water; time for a paddle in the cool water and take-out sandwiches from the corner store for lunch under a picnic table umbrella. I bought gifts—macadamia nuts and Hawaiian coffee. Then the challenge of packing everything back into a suddenly shrunken suitcase, and we drove off to the airport fot the long flight home.

BUDGET FOR A BARGAIN WEEK IN HAWAII

7 nights, B&B @ 65.00 per night	455.00
Car rental for 7 days	175.00
Meals & snacks, breakfast at B&B included	195.00
Miscellaneous (entrance fees, books, handcream)	55.00
TOTAL	$880.00

Adventure Horsepacking in Colorado

I'm riding Glishka, a sturdy Appaloosa and experienced mountain horse. Yesterday, I set off along shaded trails where aspen showed their first gold leaves, trotted across alpine meadows, and camped in Horsethief Basin.

Today, I'm climbing a narrow path above tree-level to cross South Brush Pass at 13,200 feet. I can see patches of snow on the surrounding mountains.

Huge dark clouds scud overhead. Above looms the gray mountain pass like a knife edge against the sky. Tiny hailstones bounce down, hitting my face and hat. I'm wearing sweaters, gloves, coat, and raingear. Sharp gusts of icy wind tug at my hood. The horses plod on determinedly. We're almost at the top. I'm taking deep breaths in the thin air.

I've reached the flat saddle of rock and cross the pass. Looking ahead, far, far below I see the round circles on the plains that mark fields and farms and crops, green and brown and beige. They look just the way they do when you're in a plane coming in from the east to Colorado. Circling me at eye-level, silhouetted against the sky, are the jagged peaks of the mountains like a stone necklace. Suddenly, the sun comes from behind the clouds, dazzling bright. It's as if I'm in outer space, floating in the air, detached from the earth. The view is so vast and overwhelming that no photo would do it justice. I feel an incredible sense of excitement and exhilaration.

I'm on a five-day horsepacking trip in the Sangre de Cristo Mountains, west of Colorado Springs. Glishka, a name meaning eagle in Sioux, expertly picks her way down the far side of the pass. The slope is almost vertical. She

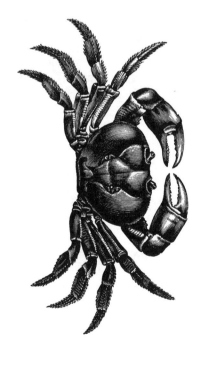

navigates the trail of loose rocks and stones, and turns steadily at the sharp zigzag corners that swivel across the rock face. I lean well back, almost standing in the stirrups to keep my balance, and trust her to know the way.

Behind me are the others: Kathryn Wickstrom, a travel consultant from California and experienced horse-owner and rider, who persuaded her father, Mike Isetta, a retired Teamster, to come along though he hasn't been riding in years; Randy Peese, a power plant worker, and Jay Reznick, a pediatric dentist, from Pennsylvania, Easterners who both ride Western-style every week; and Mary Ellen Peek, a horse trainer from Dripping Springs, Texas, who's brought photographs of herself show-jumping on her favorite horse. Turns out that we're all married, but our spouses aren't enthusiastic about adventurous riding.

I reach the bottom and dismount. I'm standing in a rolling meadow dotted with purple and white flowers. It's so lush and green that it's hard to believe high snowdrifts cover the Sangre de Cristo passes for most of the year. Only from mid-July to mid-September can you ride here where elk and deer roam, wildflowers abound, the weeping thistle blooms, and marmots, beaver, and chipmunks scurry. The trip will cross five passes over 13,000 feet, hear coyotes howl at night, fish in icy streams, and see hummingbirds and beaver.

I'm riding with Adventure Specialists, out of Bear Basin Ranch in Westcliffe. Carol Abraham and Bill Brown, the leaders, are both experts in high country riding. For five days riding, the price is around $600, including everything. An added bonus on this trip is Stephane Guyomard, a French chef-turned-cowboy, who loves to cook in the open.

On the first night, Stephane whipped fresh lobsters out of his bag, their claws flailing in the air. Cracking the shells expertly, he extracted the meat, and mixed it with the fresh scallops and shrimp in a bowl. Next he whipped up a delicate cream sauce, prepared the pasta, and tossed everything together in a large wok, balanced on the metal grill over the open fire. From another bag, a salad of fresh spinach with hearts of palm and a herb dressing appeared just as the pasta was ready, and he offered us a choice of two white wines.

Around the campfire, the "oohs" and "aahs" from the six of us were a constant refrain between mouthfuls. For dessert, Stephane produced two baked pieces, strawberry and peach, cappucino, coffee and tea. However, we did eat off paper plates and drink the wine from plastic mugs, to show we were really in the wilderness.

Every meal was a delight: grilled melt-in-the-mouth steaks, potatoes with fresh leeks and onions, broccoli with hearts of palm, grilled chicken breasts in fresh squeezed lemon juice with capers and cream, couscous with sauté-d zucchini and red peppers, carrots in orange honey glaze, rice with fresh rosemary, and pound cake topped with warm raspberry sauce.

You can request special diets on the trip. One couple asked for the no-fat Pritikin diet, and "By the end of the week, they were begging for a bit of bacon," Stephane grinned. He grew up in Paris, France, and learned to cook in his father's restaurant. After working in city restaurants in Montreal and the United States for several years, he met Carol and persuaded her to let him cook for her trips. Now he creates gourmet meals over a camp fire with pans blackened from smoke, water from the streams, and supplies loaded on a packhorse in waterproof bags.

It was easy to fall into horse-packing routine. After breakfast, we'd take down our tents, pack everything into duffles, untie the picketed horses, brush and saddle them, load bags on the four pack-horses, and fill our waterbottles (at this altitude I learned it's vital to drink lots of water to stop dehydration). As the sun warmed the mountain tops, and melted the night's frost, the line of horses set out on the trail.

On the third day, I followed the muddy trail to Cotton Lake, 12,000 feet high. Ahead, I glimpsed the smooth still blue waters of the lake. It's an oasis of peacefulness, surrounded by mountains dusted with patches of snow. Tall pine trees stretched up the slopes around the lake to be reflected in the mirror-smooth surface of the water. A beaver surfaced suddenly, and swam in a wide circle, eyeing the intruders. The sounds of birds echoed in the emptiness. Suddenly, a hummingbird flew right in front of me and quivered dramatically at my red jacket before darting away. I hiked round to the far side to sit in the warm sunshine on a rock, absorbing the peace and tranquility of the surroundings. The sun shone down from a perfect arc of blue above. The stillness was tangible.

The campsite that night overlooked Rito Alto Creek. I walked away from the campfire to look up at the vast curve of sky, where millions of stars sparkled and winked. A full moon rose like a great round globe of silver.

A rest day broke the riding routine. Jay and Randy went on a short ride to a lake nearby with Bill, Mary Ellen and I hiked up to a patch of snow and threw snowballs, Carol washed her hair in the ice-cold stream, and Mike and Kathryn went fishing to return triumphant with a dozen perfect trout. Stephane grilled them over the fire, and as we sat eating, Jay said; "I don't think I can ever take another pack trip because this one is so incredible nothing else will ever be as good." We laughed, but we knew what he meant.

The fifth day's route was challenging, even for experienced riders. The trail led across three passes: Rito Alto at 13,795', San Isabel at 13,100', and Venable at 13,600'. Riding over the first two was straightforward. The horses panted up the steep trails as I looked out awe-struck at the spectacular views. It was nearly noon when Glishka started up the zigzag trail to Venable Pass.

At the top, Bill rode through first. Then he stopped. So did the horses following him. I thought they'd paused to admire the scenery. As Glishka trotted determinedly up the final scramble to the ridge, I was hit by a fierce wind blowing like a hurricane, almost tugging me out of the saddle.

Bill shouted against the incredible noise of the wind for us to dismount, send our horses down the trail first, and follow them. I was fighting against the incredible gusts to keep my balance on the narrow trail. But Glishka didn't understand. She and three of the other horses scurried up the mountain slope to nibble at the grass. The wind was blowing so wildly I couldn't hear what Bill was shouting. He waved down the trail vigorously.

I managed to follow Randy down behind two pack horses. I could see Mary Ellen trying to keep her horse on the trail and not lose her elegant cowboy hat in the wind. Carol was struggling to stop her horse and the packhorse escaping up the mountain. Finally, with the wind tugging and howling around us, we managed to get all the horses back on to the trail, reorganized, and remounted. I rode down along narrow paths and round sharp bends, the wind howling in indignation, until suddenly the gusts stopped. An hour later, we reached the calm of a picnic spot by an abandoned barn, and stopped to catch our breath in relief.

Ahead lay the trail down to civilization. Glishka walked carefully across streams, trotted along rocky trails, and through a dazzling grove of aspen transformed into golden yellow brightness. Suddenly, I turned the corner to see a familiar parking lot with a van and horse-trailers. I tied Glishka up, said goodbye, and patted her neck. She looked away; after all, she'd be climbing mountain trails again. Only for me, the ride was over.

COLORADO RIDING TRIPS

AWE! American Wilderness Experience. P.O. Box 1486, Boulder, CO. 80306 offers dozens of adventure vacations including horsepacking trips. Call 800-444-0099. *(See page 83.)*

What If Something Goes Wrong?

On the eighth day of a river rafting trip down the Colorado River through some of the most breath-taking and spectacular Grand Canyon scenery, I tripped on a rock and cut my leg. Along the way I had successfully rafted some of the wildest rapids I have ever seen where waves soared above and crashed fiercely on our bouncing vessels. I had climbed up narrow rocky trails to peer into ancient Anasazi granaries hundreds of feet up sheer cliffs. I had scrambled over rocks and boulders in dry side canyons to find petroglyphs on rock walls and hidden waterfalls cascading into vivid greenery.

I know that statistics show that you're at risk for an accident any time you get into a car and start driving. Statistics and hospital emergency rooms attest to the fact that most accidents happen at home. But you do worry what will happen if you have an accident or get sick on vacation at some desolate place in the wilds. Well, that's exactly what happened to me.

The canyon trip I had chosen was run by expert boat people. On the first day they taught us the essential rules of safety, which we all followed. Visitors often underestimate the power and vastness of the Grand Canyon. This is not a Disneyland excursion, carefully sanitized and predictable. The Grand Canyon National Park is about 190 miles long, the distance from New York to Boston, and covers about 1,900 square miles, which includes 277 miles of the Colorado River. The canyon walls reach to about 7,000 feet above sea level at the rim.

People who walk or tour the Canyon rim may develop medical problems because of the altitude. Some elderly people can experience heart attacks and breathing problems.

Others start down the steep trails from the rim to the canyon floor without realizing how difficult it's going to be coming up again and over-exert themselves in the hot dry air.

The canyon is so vast no one has ever explored it all. From the South Rim Village you can walk along trails at the edge, look down to a drop of almost a mile, and watch the mules trotting steadily up and down the narrow trails. You can hike down to the canyon floor, but it's not an easy route, and even hike across the canyon if you're well prepared.

I decided the best way to see the canyon was to take a 13-day raft trip through the center of the Canyon on the Colorado River, just as John Wesley Powell did on his explorations more than 100 years ago. I also chose a company that offered paddle and oar rafts, not motorized, so I could appreciate the natural sounds of the Canyon. For our group of 19, there were five experienced boat guides, four men and one woman, and we set off from Lee's Feery to float about 225 miles down the river.

The waters were calm and rippling as we paddled our way down river, manoeuvering out of swirling eddies that trapped the rafts in backwaters. We learned to guide the rafts through the white-topped waves of the rapids, paddling energetically on one side or the other as our leader shouted orders from the back. The canyon walls changed from red to ocher to dark gray as we descended. One afternoon we played volleyball under the rock roof of a deep cavern. On a silent hike along the dried up river bed of a canyon, the sound of the rushing water faded behind us as we walked over rocks and boulders, the sunlight hardly reaching us over the high walls, the air calm and still.

Every evening the tents were erected on the flattest surface we could find. It might be a sandy beach, where we had to be sure to keep away from the water line which might suddenly rise depending on the Glen Canyon Dam. Since the Colorado is now a controlled flow, it's very cold (from 47 to 60 degrees F), and when there's a change in the demand for electricity, the river flow rises or falls. Other nights we picked rocky shelves amid the boulders, or smoothed down pebbles, or sheltered by shrubs and bushes. The boatmen slept on their boats, rocking on the river as the current rushed over the rocks, hurrying unceasingly. The portapotty was carefully set up to give sitters the best view of the scenery while providing maximum privacy.

Every day we enjoyed delicious meals; breakfasts with pancakes and pineapple, lunch along the river with sandwiches and salads, and dinners with steak, fresh fish and angelfood cake for desserts.

For excitement we had the rapids—some of the largest I've ever seen—and the rattlesnake that someone found by his tent, and two scorpions scuttling among the rocks. Then I tripped on the rock.

The day I fell over, we had safely reached a wide beach, with sharp-edged Schist Rocks that jutted up from the surface. I was helping to pull in a boat, when I tripped and fell on a rock, and said "Schist" for obvious reasons. A guide brought out a first aid kit, and since we happened to have four nurses in the group, they all stood around and gave advice. The cut was thoroughly cleaned to remove all the sand, doused with disinfectant, and wrapped in pristine white bandages. It was deep, but not painful, and it didn't look as if it had hit the bone.

I considered how I could cope for the rest of the trip, with the rapids, the camping, and the water. The nurses and the guides were concerned that it would be very difficult to keep the wound dry and clean, and if dirt got in, it could get infected. We agreed I should get out and see a doctor. But there I was, a mile down the deepest canyon in the world, a deep cut on my leg under a big white bandage, no trails out, no way of getting upstream, and three days from the end of the trip. What could I do?

No problem. The raft guides whipped out a radio from the bottom of one of the rafts and tinkered with wires and plugs until it was operating. Then we waited for one of the cross-country planes to fly over the Grand Canyon. Why? The system is simple. When a plane flies over the area, the crew sends out an emergency message. The plane relays it to the tower of the Los Angeles airport which sends it to Prescott Tower in Phoenix, Arizona, and it's sent to the Grand Canyon Park emergency center. The planes can locate where the signal comes from, and know the canyon well enough to recognize different places. Many places in the canyon can contact the Ranger Station at Phantom Ranch. But if you're down by the river, hemmed in by rock walls, you have to send your message upwards.

Grand Canyon's Emergency Medical Clinic is prepared for accidents. Almost three million people visit the Grand Canyon every year, and more than 1,500 require emergency medical aid of some kind from National Park Service rangers.

Within half an hour, just as the last rays of the sun were leaving the canyon walls, the crew had received a radio reply from the emergency center. Because it was getting dark, they asked if the injured person was in a life-threatening situation or could wait until morning when it would be safer to fly into the canyon. We decided I could stay the night and be picked

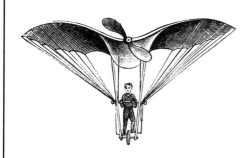

up in the morning. So I relaxed on a comfortably padded sleeping bag, my leg propped up on several life jackets, while everyone took photographs. After a dinner by the campfire, one of the boatmen played his guitar. Under the sparkling brilliance of the stars, I drifted off to sleep.

Next morning, just as the first rays of sunshine lit the sky, I heard the sound of a helicopter reverberating in the air. The whirling propeller appeared over the cliffs. Spotting our camp, the helicopter flew upriver to land on a flat piece of rocky shore. Two medics scrambled down to check me out. I said I could walk - or hop - to the plane, so they didn't need to bring a stretcher. Holding on to one of the river guides, we set off over the pebbly beach. I finally had to accept a piggyback ride to cross the stream but we made it to the helicopter. I climbed in, and was strapped into the seat. Then we took off, soaring up into the air, the tents shrinking below us. The wide rushing river became a narrow grey stream as we moved vertically up the canyon walls. We flew over the miles of flat plateau dotted with dry bushes and bare rocks that hides the dramatic canyons. Suddenly we were over buildings, roads, civilization. The helicopter landed and I hopped out into an ambulance to take me to the clinic on the South Rim.

The doctor was waiting. A nurse gave my leg an X-ray. The bone wasn't broken, but the cut was deep. The doctor sewed it up carefully with 12 neat stitches, we chatted about hikes, rafting, and the canyon. I gave them my leaflet about the trip because they said they'd like to take one!

That night I relaxed at a hotel in Flagstaff, courtesy of the rafting company. The next day I flew home, taking advantage of the wheelchair service at the airport so I didn't have to walk for miles down corridors. My own doctor checked the cut, and said it looked fine. Today, I can't even find the V-shaped scar on my leg that interrupted my Grand Canyon adventure, though I still have the memories of a very exciting adventure vacation.

For a list of companies that take rafting trips down the Grand Canyon, contact:
Grand Canyon National Park,
PO Box 129,
Grand Canyon AZ 86023
Phone: 602-638-7888

What to pack for a river rafting adventure

"Wet" is the operative word on a river trip. Everything can—and often does—get soaked. Leave anything valuable at home; it might fall into the water. Wrap cameras in plastic bags or invest in a waterproof camera. Pack all your gear in a duffle bag or laundry bag. Waterproof it by putting a large plastic trash bag inside first and then put your gear inside. The large bag will not be accessible during the day while you're on the boat, so pack your camera, candy, gum, and other small items in a ditty bag or small day pack, also waterproofed. The secret is to take less stuff, and have more fun.

Clothes
1 wet suit (if it's cool)
1 pair wet suit booties to wear in boat
2 pairs tennis shoes or river sandals
1 pair jeans or jogging suit
1 pair shorts
2 long sleeved shirts
1 warm sweater
T-shirts
1 bathing suit
1 warm jacket - fleece is good.
Handkerchief or bandana
Hat with string
Raincoat, poncho or rain suit
2 pairs socks
Underwear
Long underwear leggings

Personal
Sleeping bag
Pillow
Towel
Air mattress, foam pad
Lightweight tent
Flashlight
Suncreen, lip balm, suntan lotion, skin cream.
Medication
Insect repellant
Soap & shampoo biodegradable.
Daypack/ditty bag
Ziplock plastic bags to keep things dry.
Musical instrument
Water bottle
Roll toilet paper

ORGANIZATIONS A TO Z

The following listings tell you exactly where to find your perfect volunteer or bargain adventure vacation. Every listing has been carefully checked for accuracy by the organizations. Here in one place is all the essential information you need. You'll find name, address, phone, fax, and contact person as well as information on costs, number of programs, age range, if children are welcome, major emphasis of the programs, sample programs, and exactly what is provided.

List of Organizations

Adirondack Mountain Club
Adventure Bound River Expeditions
Alaska Chugach National Forest
Alaska River Journeys
Alaska State Parks
Alaska Wildland Adventures
Alpine Skills International
American Hiking Society
Appalachian Mountain Club
Arizona - Navajo National Monument
Arizona - Passport in Time
Arizona Raft Adventures
Arkansas - Hot Springs National Park
Arkansas - Ouachita National Forest
AWE! American Wilderness Experience
Backroads
California Departmentt of Parks & Recreation
California - Lake Tahoe Basin
California - Passport in Time
California - Sequoia National Parks
Canoe Country Escapes
Canyonlands Field Institute
Caretta Turtle Research Project
Colorado Dude & Guest Ranch Assn
Colorado - Mesa Verde National Park
Colorado - Pike/San Isabel National Forests
Colorado State Parks Volunteers
Colorado Trail Foundation
Country Inns Along the Trail
Country Walkers

Craftsbury Running Camps
Crater of Diamonds State Park
Crow Canyon Archaeological Center
Desert Survivors
Dinamation International Society
Dirt Camp for Mountain Bikers
Earthwatch
Florida - Everglades National Park
Florida State Parks
Glacier Institute
Gold Vacations - Colorado
Gold Vacations - Georgia
Hawaii - Haleakala National Park
Hostelling International/AYH
Idaho - Panhandle National Forest
Idaho - Passport in Time
Indiana - Wayne National Forest
International Wolf Center
Massachusetts Audubon Society
Michigan - Isle Royale National Park
Michigan - Passport in Time
Minnesota - Voyageurs National Park
Montana - Little Bighorn Battlefield
Montana - Passport in Time
Mountain Travel-Sobek
National Audubon Society
National Wildlife Federation
Natural Habitat
Nature Expeditions International
New Mexico - Carlsbad Caverns Natl Park
New Mexico - Passport in Time
North Carolina - Blue Ridge Parkway
North Cascades Institute
Ohio Department of Natural Resources
Olympic Park Institute
Oregon - Bureau of Land Management
Oregon - Deschutes National Forest
Oregon - Passport in Time
Pacific Catalyst
Paragon Guides
Passport in Time
Pennsylvania State Parks
Pocono Environmental Education Center
Potomac Appalachian Trail Club
Roads Less Traveled
Rocky Mountain Nature Association
Saga Holidays

Sierra Club Service Trips
Smithsonian Study Tours
Student Conservation Association
Sundance Expeditions & Kayak School
Texas - Aransas National Wildlife Refuge
Timberline Bicycle Tours
University Research Expeditions Program
Utah Bureau of Land Management
Utah - Canyonlands National Park
Utah - Passport in Time
Vermont State Parks
Victor Emanuel Nature Tours
Victory Chimes Windjammer Cruises
Virginia Dept of Conservation
Virginia - George Washington National Forest
Volunteers for Outdoor Colorado
Volunteers for Outdoor Washington
Volunteers for Peace
Wisconsin - Apostle Islands National Lakeshore
Wisconsin Dept of Natural Resources
Wyoming - Bridger/Teton National Forest
Wyoming Bureau of Land Management
Yellowstone Institute
Zoetic Research & Sea Quest Expeditions

Adirondack Mountain Club (ADK)

Address: PO Box 867, Lake Placid, NY 12946
Phone: 518-523-3480
Fax: 518-523-3518
Contact: Trails Office

Cost:
FREE. Donations requested. Non-profit organization.
Number of programs:
30.
Age range:
16 to 80.
Children:
No.
Major emphasis:
Trail maintenance and reconstruction that is inherently educational.
Sample programs:
Trail projects from one to five days.
Trail maintenance skills workshop.
Special projects such as National Trails Day.
Provides:
Accommodations, guides, equipment, instruction, pre-trip material, all meals, transportation on land.

Spend a few days in a region of rolling mountains and spectacular views in New York state while you help ADK keep 2,000 miles of trails in the Adirondack and Catskill Mountains in good shape. You work with experienced leaders, enthusiastic volunteers, and learn from the experts how to do trail work right.

On arrival at base camp, your leader directs you to your space, usually in a tent already set up. The chuckwagon, a fully stocked kitchen, provides all meals, cooked by the group. That evening, you receive a detailed orientation on what needs to be done. All tools are provided, and the emphasis is on safety, health, and low-impact camping techniques.

The next morning, the crew leader divides up the tools and food among the group, and a van brings the crew to the trailhead. There's a hike to a new campsite which is set up for the week. The leader tells everyone exactly what needs to be accomplished, and it's off to work along the trail.

Challenging projects include installing drainage and building an outhouse. You may work on tread hardening, or clear encroaching brush off trails. Projects vary and there's always one easy project for first-timers or seniors. ADK also offers free workshops on basic trail maintenance after which you can join the Adopt-A-Trail program in the Adirondack Park.

In 1994, 224 ADK volunteers completed 4,792 hours of trail work. They built 50 rock steps, 61 step stones, 346 feet of bog bridge construction, and completed 21 miles of blowdown removal, 26 miles of sidecutting, and 510 feet of new drainage.

Adventure Bound River Expeditions

Address: 2392 H Road, Grand Junction, CO 81505
Phone: 1-800-423-4668 in US & Canada
Fax: 970-241-5633
Contact: Tom Kleinschnitz

Since 1963, Adventure Bound has offered trips through some of the most beautiful canyon country in Utah and Colorado. The river trips are designed for beginners and more experienced rafters. One participant has taken annual trips with the company for 16 years, first with his children, and now with his grandchildren.

You can choose a one-day excursion or a five-day camping trip down a variety of rivers. On the upper Green River the boats pass through the magnificent scenery of Desolation and Gray canyons. You can float through Westwater Canyon on the Colorado, on the Green River through Dinosaur National Monument, and down the Yampa, one of the last untouched major wild rivers that swells with spring run-off. More challenging rapids are found in Cataract Canyon. You travel in pontoon rafts, oar rafts, and paddle boats. There are also inflatable canoes for those who want to try paddling on their own along the way.

There's a unique 19-day trip in May from Deerlodge to Hite Marina on Lake Powell, following the Yampa, Green, and Colorado rivers on the high water snow melt, through more than 400 miles of wilderness and hundreds of rapids.

Cost:
Trips range from $75 to $650. Tents and camping kits can be rented for $35 each.

Number of programs:
Five different rivers and about 160 trips.

Age range:
6 to 90.

Children:
8 and up welcome on Lodore and Desolation trips.

Major emphasis:
River rafting, inflatable kayaks, and participation.

Sample programs:
Westwater Canyon, 1-day trip, $98. *Green River & Dinosaur National Monument*, 3-day trip, $410. *Desolation & Grey Canyons*, 5-day trip, $660.

Provides:
Camping accommodation, guides, equipment, all meals, transportation on land. Youth and group rates available.

"I have been on 25 to 30 trips with this one company! Tom Kleinschnitz does a great job of having his boat men and women hit the center of the rapids for the best possible ride."
Participant from Colorado

Alaska - Chugach National Forest

Address: Cordova Ranger District, PO Box 280, Cordova, AK 99574
Phone: 907-424-7661
Contact: Dana Smyke

The Chugach National Forest/Cordova District is on the eastern side of Prince William Sound. It's an isolated region without roads to interior Alaska, so planes and boats are the only way to travel. There's daily air service, and a ferry boat service about five times a week.

Every year the USDA Forest Service has openings for assistants. You can serve on the trail crew to maintain about 30 miles of existing trails in the Cordova Ranger District Trail System. You can help maintain 18 public cabins throughout the region with free housing plus $20 a day. If you stay 60 days or more, you receive free transportation from Seattle to Cordova plus a return flight.

You can serve as a Forest Service Host at a glacier recreation area, where you'll camp free at a remote site, or bring your own RV or trailer. A round-trip ferry ticket from Valdez to Cordova is provided free.

In the summer Cordova's population swells to 5,000 people, but only half as many stay there during the winter. The nearby Copper River Delta is a major breeding and staging area for millions of shorebirds and waterfowl, and you may see moose, brown bear, and wolves.

Cost:
FREE.
Number of programs:
Several.
Age range:
Over 18.
Children:
No.
Major emphasis:
Service projects.
Sample programs:
Trail Crew for construction and repair. *Cabin Maintenance*, carpentry helpful. *Forest Service Hosts* at Child's Glacier Recreation Area.
Provides:
Accommodations, propane, gas for generator, water. $20 a day on cabin project.
ALSO
Alaska State Parks have openings for Campground Hosts in 12 State Parks in the Chugach area, at campgrounds and day use recreation sites.

Alaska River Journeys

Address: PO Box 220204, Anchorage, AK 99522
Phone: 907-349-2964
Fax: 907-349-2964
Contact: Steve Weller

"Our goal is to guide you safely and comfortably through Alaska on some of North America's last remaining wild and scenic river corridors," explains Steve Weller, who with co-director Brenda Roper has over 35 years of outdoor experience. They have been running rivers in Alaska since 1985, including the Aniakchak, Gulkana, Tikchik, and Sheenjek which lies above the Arctic Circle.

From Anchorage, you can float the Kenai River, sea kayak along the coast of Resurrection Bay, and take the Alaska Railroad back. You can mountain bike and raft along the border of Wrangell-St. Elias National Park, fly via floatplane to Kenai Lake, or spend five days on the Gulkana River fishing and looking for caribou.

Camps range from wide gravel beaches with blossoming wildflowers to riverside sites with great views of Alaska's mountains, and soft tundra. Meals include home-baked breads, gourmet menus, and delicious desserts.

Cost:
From $225 to $3,445.
Number of programs:
About 20.
Age range:
12 and up.
Children:
Best age: over 11.
Major emphasis:
Wilderness travel and discovery.
Sample programs:
Tazlina River camp/raft, 3 days, $775. *Mountain bike, raft & sail*, 7 days, $1,595. *Tikchik River raft/ fish*, 7 days, $2,745.
Provides:
Airfare within Alaska, accommodations, excursions, guides, equipment, all meals, transportation.

"An unforgettable introduction to the beauty of being on a river. Great food, great service, and great scenery!"
Participant from Michigan

Alaska State Parks

Address: **Department of Natural Resources**
Division of Parks & Outdoor Recreation
3601 C Street, Suite 1200, Anchorage, AK 99503-5921
Phone: **907-762-2612**
Fax: **907-762-2535**
Contact: **Volunteer Coordinator**

Alaska State Parks has about 60 volunteer Campground Host positions statewide, from Kodiak to Fairbanks to Ketchikan. You can stay on Quartz Lake (which has the best rainbow and silver salmon fishing in the interior), or in the upland forest and tundra of the Chena River area, or amid the spectacular scenery of Denali State Park at Byers Lake Campground at the foot of Kesugi Ridge with views of Mt. McKinley.

Hosts welcome campers, explain park facilities and regulations, answer questions, and help visitors plan their trips. They also help park rangers with the daily operation and maintenance of campgrounds, and do light maintenance work. The season runs from mid-May to mid-September, and a few places are open longer.

Volunteers can apply for as many positions as they like by filling in the detailed volunteer application forms. Popular positions are filled early, so apply as early as possible before the April 1 deadline.

The Volunteers in Parks program needs campground hosts, and some 60 other positions that include research projects for college interns, trail crews, ranger assistants in back-country locations, and at historical sites.

Cost:
FREE.
Number of programs:
Several.
Age range:
Over 18.
Children:
No.
Major emphasis:
Service projects.
Sample programs:
Campground Hosts. Historic Site Assistants. Backcountry Ranger Assistants.
Provides:
Campsite, use of facilities, training, uniforms. Sometimes food stipend.

Alaska Wildland Adventures

Address: PO Box 389, Girdwood AK 99587
Phone: 800-334-8730: 907-783-2928
Contact: Kirk Hoessle, Director

"Don't try to see too much in Alaska, but spend quality time at the places you visit," advises Kirk Hoessle. "You should want to leave Alaska with its true essence - close encounters with wildlife, an appreciation for the harshness of this northern environment that helps keep this country wild, and the magic and realities of life in the Last Frontier."

A variety of Alaska adventures for seniors, families, and singles are offered by this experienced company, in business since 1977. You choose the tour you'd prefer: tent camping, cabin stays, a mixture of tent and cabin, or lodge and cabins. You can go for a few days, a week or longer. All trips visit remote and relatively natural environments, using low impact travel, and there's a strong educational emphasis so that travelers learn about the natural and cultural history of the places they visit. The Senior Safari offers more comforts and less strenuous activity.

The range of activities is varied. You can raft the Kenai river and explore the Kenai National Wildlife Refuge and Skilak Lake. A boat tour takes you to Kenai Fjords National Park where you see huge glaciers, sea otters, puffins, and seals. You can flightsee over Mt. McKinley. You tour Denali National Park to see caribou, grizzlies, and moose, and spend a day hiking and photographing in the park. Special off-season trips and fishing safaris are also available.

The company has designed a set of eco-tourism guidelines to help travelers respect the environment, and participants can volunteer a Dollar A Day for Conservation based on the cost of their tour.

Cost:
From $711 to $3,395.
Number of programs:
About 14.
Age range:
All ages.
Children:
Yes, especially on family trips.
Major emphasis:
Alaska wilderness vacations.
Sample programs:
Penzli Backcountry Lodge, 3 nights, $711. *Campout Adventure*, 10 days, $1,895. *Senior Safari*, 8 days, $2,550.
Provides:
Accommodations, all meals, excursions, guides, equipment, transportation, pre-trip information. Airfares in Alaska not included.

"Being in each place long enough to be a part of the land through hiking, rafting, gold panning, etc., we came to really experience Alaska at a pace we could enjoy."
Participants from Texas

Alpine Skills International

Address: PO Box 8, Norden, CA 95724
Phone: 916-426-9108
Contact: Bela or Mimi

Cost:
From $55 to $3,280.
Number of programs:
More than 100.
Age range:
All ages, active people.
Children:
No.
Major emphasis:
Education and new techniques for mountain skiers and climbers.
Sample programs:
Rock Climbing/Beginning, 2 days, $138. *Telemark and Nordic Downhill* I & II, 3 days, $198. *High Sierra Ski Tour,* 6 days, $542.
Provides:
Accommodations, some meals (depends on program), guides, instruction, transportation. Rental equipment available.

You ski through the fresh snow of the Sierra Mountains and discover how to stay warm and comfortable on an overnight ski tour on a weekend *Introduction to Ski Camping* course. Or, you can choose a three-day seminar and learn high-tech ski camping skills that will enable you to join longer ski-touring expeditions. The ASI was founded by two experienced skiers and climbers in 1979, and provides a range of programs that improve skills and develop new abilities for skiers and climbers.

"We urge everyone to go through the steps they need to at their own pace," the directors advise. "Don't be in a hurry. Have goals but learn to understand the value of the experience along the way. Teach others to be gentle to the mountain environment."

Ski programs for weekend and week-long excursions cover cross-country skiing, telemark, backcountry skiing, avalanche seminars, navigation skills, Nordic downhill skiing, and ski tours along the High Sierra Route.

Beginning rock climbers learn the techniques of movement on rock, how to handle the rope, tie necessary knots, anchor belays, and rappel safely. More advanced programs cover rescue, rock anchoring, crack climbing, high altitude mountaineering, and snow climbing among other topics, as well as expeditions to climb the high peaks in the Sierras.

American Hiking Society

Address: PO Box 20160, Washington, DC 20041-2160
Phone: 703-255-9304
Contact: Susan Henley or Chuck Kines

Absolutely free vacations in the outdoors are offered through AHS, a trail education and advocacy group. Complete details of hundreds of volunteer opportunities in a national or state park, forest or public land are described in *Helping in the Outdoors*, the AHS annual directory ($7).

There are dozens of openings for campground hosts and trail crews, but there are also opportunities for graphic artists, geologists, biologists, carpenters, computer and data entry experts, gardeners, historians, hydrologists, librarians, surveyors and more.

AHS also organizes its own Volunteer Vacations program. Teams go into the backcountry to spend ten days on projects ranging from trail maintenance in Texas to bridge building in Wyoming, and similar outdoor efforts in Hawaii, Alaska, New Hampshire, California, Montana, and Arizona. Most sites are in remote, primitive areas, and participants should be experienced hikers and physically able to backpack and work hard.

Cost:
FREE. Nonprofit organization. Registration fee: $50.

Number of programs:
58.

Age range:
18 and over.

Children:
No.

Major emphasis:
Preserving parks and forests.

Sample programs:
Bridge building, Wyoming. *Trail clearing*, Texas. *Fence repair*, New Hampshire.

Provides:
Food, tools, training, transportation. Participants bring tent, sleeping bag, backpack.

"Volunteer Vacations have been especially popular with seniors and with families who want to give something back for the enjoyment they've received from the outdoors."

Susan Henley

Appalachian Mountain Club

Address: PO Box 298, Gorham, NH 03581
Phone: 603-466-2721
Fax: 603-466-2822
Contact: Judy Smith

When you hike along a trail, have you ever wondered who cleared the rocks, painted the markers along the way, and built bridges across the streams?

The Appalachian Mountain Club, founded in 1876, is the oldest and largest recreation and conservation organization in the United States, with more than 65,000 members. The club has become expert in trail restoration and preservation.

Volunteers cut back overgrown brush, repair shelters, and clear fallen trees. AMC members spend thousands of hours every year maintaining more than 1,200 miles of trails in the Northeast, including 350 miles of the Appalachian Trail. The AMC works in cooperation with the National Park Service, US Forest Service, state agencies, and other organizations and landowners on projects. Its guide, *Trail Building and Maintenance*, is nationally recognized.

You can join a one-week volunteer base camp and work on trail restoration in New York's Catskill Mountains, Mount Greylock in the Berkshires in Massachusetts, or in the White Mountains in New Hampshire. Weekend projects are also available. In New Hampshire, the AMC runs the White Mountain Hut System and Pinkham Notch Visitor Center, in cooperation with the US Forest Service. There are also several camps in New England.

AMC also provides crews for service projects in Alaska, Idaho, Maine, and Wyoming.

Costs:
From $60 to $200.
Number of programs:
Many.
Age range:
16 to 60 +. Average age: 18 to 40.
Children:
16 and over. Teen program available.
Major emphasis:
Public service on public lands.
Sample programs:
Trailclearing or Volunteer Caretaker, one week, $60. *Service Trips*, 10 or 12 days, $195. *Teen Program*, 2 weeks, $200.
Provides:
Accommodations, all meals, leaders, tools, training, some equipment.

Arizona - Navajo National Monument

Address: HC 71 Box 3, Tonalea, AZ 86044
Phone: 602-672-2366
Contact: Superintendent

This splendid site, situated at 7,300 feet in the Navajo Indian Reservation, is visited by thousands of people every year. Some drive through and stop at lookout points, and others stay to take a tour, or spend a few days camping in the campgrounds. Guided tours are offered during the summer, and there are hiking trails that lead to the monuments.

The area has some of the best preserved Kayenta Anasazi ruins in the southwest, including the ruins of Betatakin (which means "ledge house" in Navajo) and Keet Seel (which means "broken pieces of pottery" in Navajo). These date from the last half of the 13th century, when farmers once lived in these bare canyons, grew crops, built houses, and raised families. Then about 1300 AD they abandoned their homes in the cliffs and moved away. The amazing ruins of the villages they left behind are preserved in this monument.

Volunteers are needed to serve as campground and park hosts, answer visitors' questions, lead guided hikes, look after the information and sales desks, and do campground maintenance.

Cost:
   FREE.
Number of programs:
   Several.
Age range:
   Over 18.
Children:
   No.
Major emphasis:
   Service projects.
Sample programs:
   Campground Hosts. Park Hosts. Information Desk Assistants.
Provides:
   RV sites, training, uniforms, supervision. Dormitory housing and food stipends may be available.

Arizona - Passport in Time

Address: PIT Clearinghouse, PO Box 18364, Washington, DC 20036
Phone: 202-293-0922
Fax: 202-293-1782
Contact: Jill Shaefer

Cost:
  FREE.
Number of programs:
  3.
Age range:
  18 and over.
Children:
  No.
Major emphasis:
  Historic preservation.
Sample programs:
  Various archaeology projects.
Provides:
  Varies. Campsites, equipment, instruction, materials.

Passport in Time invites volunteers to enjoy free vacations while helping on a variety of historic preservation projects in Arizona.

At Clover Ruin, 33 miles west of Flagstaff, in Kaibab National Forest, volunteers continue the work of excavating a prehistoric farmstead occupied by the Cohonina people between AD 900-1000. This project involves excavating, screening, analyzing artifacts, and record-keeping. Once the original construction layout has been identified, reconstruction will begin to create an authentic-looking prehistoric farmstead for public interpretation.

Next to the rugged Granite Mountain Wilderness in Prescott National Forest, Granite Basin is a wooded area surrounded by ridges, boulders and peaks, some reaching to 7,000 feet. Here, among the ponderosa pine, is Granite Basin Lake and Campground, both built during the Depression. Archaeological work has focused on the area's prehistoric inhabitants, and work will continue on the site of an early pithouse. Volunteers have discovered ceramics, stone artifacts, and other evidence, and will continue this work.

Oxbow Hill overlooks the northern reaches of Tonto Basin in Tonto National Forest, beneath the Mogollon Rim of central Arizona. Here, prehistoric cultures existed for thousands of years, shown by the rock art that they left behind. Volunteers will help document rock art at recently identified sites, and work will include photography, mapping, and scale drawings of rock panels containing petroglyphs.

Arizona Raft Adventures

Address: 4050 East Huntington Drive, Flagstaff, AZ 86004
Phone: 1-800-786-RAFT: 602-528-8200.
Fax: 602-526-8246
Contact: Trips Director

Cost:
From $330 to $2,074.
Number of programs:
Dozens of trips down the Grand Canyon and on San Juan river.
Age range:
7 to 80.
Children:
Best age: 7 and over on San Juan; over 10 on Grand Canyon trips.
Major emphasis:
River rafting in the southwest, motor and oar.
Sample programs:
San Juan River, Bluff to Mexican Hat, 3 days, $393. *Grand Canyon, Lees Ferry to Pipe Creek*, 6 days, $1,470. *Grand Canyon, Lees Ferry to Diamond Creek*, 14 days, $2,060.
Provides:
Camping accommodation with sleeping bag, pad, liner and ground cloth, lifejackets, two waterproof bags, all meals, land transportation from Flagstaff, guides, equipment, AzRA mug, Grand Canyon guidebook, Arizona taxes, park fees.

The sun slowly climbs over the canyon cliff and peeks over the jagged edge, flooding the campsite with brilliant warm sunshine. There's a smell of coffee brewing, the sand is soft underfoot, the rushing water of the river tumbling by over rocks and stones is like a wake-up song, and above is crystal-clear air soaring in a dome of pristine blue sky.

It's a typical morning on a rafting trip. For your first trip with AzRA, start off on the relaxing waters of the San Juan River. It's a wonderful place to enjoy the pace of river life, casual picnics on beaches along the way, paddling the raft, and the relaxed camaraderie of taste-tingling dinners in the evening by the campfire, created by the guides who don't hesitate to whip up a birthday cake at a moment's notice.

AzRA specializes in trips down the Grand Canyon, which is the ultimate river experience. It's not recommended for apprehensive beginners - many of the rapids are truly wild, with huge waves. The company offers trips where you paddle the rafts, oar trips where an experienced boatman maneuvers the raft, hybrid trips with some oar and some paddle boats, and an eight-day motor trip down the entire Grand Canyon.

AzRA welcome first-timers, experienced rafters, families and the disabled, on its trips. Whichever way you choose to float down the river, it will be a memorable experience.

"I was near novice but the crew made me feel comfortable without patronizing. I was especially impressed with their love of the river and knowledge of the geology of the area."
Participant on Grand Canyon trip

"Stephen, aged 7, had a fantastic trip. He still recounts tales of his adventures to us and is very eager for all the family to take another trip."
Grandparent on San Juan trip

Arkansas - Hot Springs National Park

Address: PO Box 1860, Hot Springs, AR 71902
Phone: 501-623-1433, Ext 652
Contact: Jeff Heitzman

Famous for its 47 thermal springs, this national park covers about 5,000 acres. There are more than 30 miles of hiking trails, picnic areas, campsites, and the Hot Water Cascades. Set in the Ouachita Mountains, it's a popular place for visitors. The city of Hot Springs has hotels and sightseeing tours.

Hot Springs National Park was established in 1832 as the first federal reserve. You can tour the turn-of-the-century bathhouses that line the original Bathhouse Row.

Volunteers are welcome year-round - there's no deadline for applications. You can answer visitors' questions, help with the bookstore, or assist with computer programming and office machine operation. Campground aides are welcome to do minor maintenance and cleaning, and assist with trail work.

Cost:
FREE.
Number of programs:
Several.
Age range:
Over 18.
Children:
No.
Major emphasis:
Service projects.
Sample programs:
Campground Aides. Visitor Center Aides. Administrative Aides.
Provides:
Campsite with full hook-ups, housing may be available. Some training given.

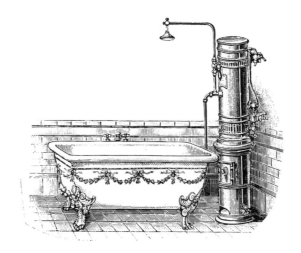

Arkansas - Ouachita National Forest

Address: Mena Ranger District, 1603 Hwy 71 N., Mena, AR 71953
Phone: 501-394-2382
Contact: Jessie Dear

Ouachita is a National Forest covering more than 1.6 million acres. It's the oldest and largest in the South. There are facilities for camping, fishing, picnicking and hiking. The National Recreation Trail stretches for 224 miles across the Forest from Talihina, Oklahoma, to Pinnacle Mountain State Park near Little Rock. From Mena, a scenic highway winds through the forests and climbs the mountains for spectacular views.

Volunteers are welcome at many of the recreation facilities. Campground hosts help at a site on a small, shady lake. Wilderness rangers stay out in the wilderness areas to help hikers and bikers along the trails, while others assist in trail maintenance.

Cost:
  FREE.
Number of programs:
  Several.
Age range:
  Over 18.
Children:
  No.
Major emphasis:
  Service projects.
Sample programs:
  Campground Hosts. Visitor Information Station Attendants. Wilderness Trail Maintenance.
Provides:
  Depends on project.

AWE! American Wilderness Experience

Address: PO Box 1486 , Boulder, CO 80306
Phone: 1-800-444-0099: 303-444-2622
Fax: 303-444-3999
Contact: Dave Wiggins, President

Cost:
From $375 to $3,395.
Number of programs:
More than 100.
Age range:
All ages.
Children:
Welcome on most trips.
Major emphasis:
Quality outdoor adventures.
Sample trips:
Snowmobile Safari, Yellowstone National Park, 4 days, $945. *Hawaii Odyssey,* 6 days, $975. *Natural History Safari, Alaska*, 10 days, $3,195.
Provides:
Accommodations, most meals, excursions, guides, equipment, instruction, pre-trip material, transportation.

A super resource for adventure vacations that take you horsepacking, whitewater rafting, backpacking, llama trekking, fishing, canoeing, sea kayaking, snowmobiling, mountain biking, cross-country skiing, and sailing.

AWE! was established in 1971, and is America's oldest and largest domestic adventure travel company. It's a clearinghouse and central reservation office for more than 100 leading outfitters and ranches in the United States, and also arranges trips for specific groups. Their dude ranch brochure lists dozens of places to stay in Colorado, Utah, Montana, Wyoming, and Arizona, where you can play cowboy, go hiking, and square dance in the evenings. Other trips take you salmon fishing in Alaska, river rafting down the Snake River in Idaho, and canoeing in the Minnesota Boundary Waters.

In winter, there's a 13-day visit to the "real" Hawaii - where you laze on sun-filled beaches, hike tree-shaded jungle trails, snorkel and swim in warm, glass-clear waters, trek over the moonscape rocks of still-smoking Kilauea Volcano and feast at an authentic luau celebration with flowery leis and hula dancing. Try a week's sea kayaking in Baja California, take a snowmobile tour of Yellowstone National Park, or lope through Superstition Wilderness in Arizona on a luxury horsepacking trip.

AWE! welcomes beginners: "The majority of our guests are first-timers themselves! Our seasoned guides and wranglers will offer as much instruction and guidance as needed."

"In virtually every way the trip was everything I had hoped for, and then some." Participant from New York

Backroads

Address: 1516 5th Street, Berkeley, CA 94710-1740
Phone: 1-800-462-2848; 510-527-1555
Fax: 510-527-1444
Contact: Director

Costs:
From $698 to $1,698.
Number of programs:
Hundreds of bike trips, dozens of walking trips.
Age range:
All ages.
Children:
Any age for family trips. Other: over 6, camping trips; over 12 on inn trips.
Major emphasis:
Active travel programs.
Sample programs:
Coastal Bike Ride, Maine, 5 days, camping, $698. *Walking Zion & Bryce Canyon National Parks*, 6 days, camping, $738. *Biking California Redwood Empire*, 5 days, inns, $1,245.
Provides:
Accommodations, all meals, safety helmet, support van, tour guides. Lightweight 21-speed bikes can be rented from the company.

Affordable walking and hiking, biking, cross-country skiing, and running vacations in the USA and abroad are offered by this company established in 1979. Its colorful brochures describe hundreds of trips for beginners, intermediates, and experts. Sampler Vacations offer the opportunity to try two or three different activities. There's a choice of elegant inns or carefully selected hotels, or camping in well-equipped tents with excellent meals.

A week's walking inn tour in California Wine Country begins on the historical plaza of Sonoma where you stay in a hotel with four-poster beds and balconies. You visit Jack London State Park, Kenwood Vineyards, an ancient redwood forest, Napa Valley vineyards, and spend two nights in a hotel in Calistoga before returning to Sonoma.

A hiking tour in Montana's Glacier National Park offers inns or campsites. Hikes take you along Avalanche Gorge to the lake, and you drive to the top of Logan Pass on Going-to-the-Sun Road. Other hikes take you to Glacier Park, Iceberg Lake, Two Medicine Lake, and views of the Continental Divide.

Backroads offers hundreds of bike trips. You can go to Alaska, Washington, Oregon and California; to New Mexico's spectacular canyon parks, the Rocky Mountains and Yellowstone National Park; Kentucky, Louisiana, and Mississippi; and Maine, Vermont, Maryland, and Martha's Vineyard on the east coast.

Bikers stop for interesting sights: a stroll through Santa Fe's museums and art galleries, a ride on a narrow-gauge railroad in the Colorado Rockies, deep sea fishing off the Kona coast of Hawaii. You camp or stay in hotels and inns. Participants need ride only as far as they want, and can hop into the support van when tired. Trips are rated for Beginners, Energetic Beginners, Intermediates, or Advanced with a realistic description of the terrain.

California Department of Parks & Recreation

Address: North Coast Redwoods District, 600-A,
West Clark, Eureka, CA 95501
Phone: 707-445-6547
Contact: Alan Wilkinson

California's vast redwood parks contain the tallest trees in the world, some more than 300 feet high. The Coastal Redwood Belt extends for 500 miles in northern California, but the best specimens of trees are found in the counties of Del Norte, Humboldt, Mendocino, and Sonoma. The Redwoods National Park Center is in Orick.

The North Coast Redwoods District is one of 12 Redwoods State Park districts along California's north coast from the Oregon border to the town of Leggett some 250 miles south. They are responsible for 21 park units, and welcome assistants as campground hosts and park volunteers, to work in visitor centers or assist on hiking trails and maintenance projects.

Cost:
FREE.
Number of programs:
Several.
Age range:
Over 18.
Children:
No.
Major emphasis:
Redwood parks preservation.
Sample programs:
Assist at visitor centers and campgrounds.
Provides:
Depends on park.

California - Lake Tahoe Basin

Address: Lake Tahoe Basin Management, 870 Emerald Bay Rd # 1, S. Lake Tahoe, CA 96150
Phone: 916-573-2600
Contact: Michael St. Michel

Lake Tahoe is the largest and deepest alpine lake on the North American continent set 6,227 feet high amid the snow-capped Sierra Nevada peaks. Lake Tahoe averages 274 sunny days a year, and an annual snowfall of 25 to 40 feet.

In winter, there's downhill and cross-country skiing, snowmobiling and sledding. In summer visitors cruise the lake in paddlewheelers and sailboats, or go waterskiing, though the water is cool for swimming. They also enjoy the trails for biking, hiking, and horseriding.

You will find plenty of openings for volunteers at a variety of different sites during the summer, and must apply by April 1. You can serve as an interpretive naturalist and talk to visitors, help with historical or archaeological projects, or serve on trails as a wilderness ranger, among other opportunities.

Cost:
FREE.
Number of programs:
Several.
Age range:
Over 18.
Children:
No.
Major emphasis:
Service projects.
Sample programs:
Restoration-Cultural Interpretation, Tallac Historic Site. *Interpretive Naturalists. Wilderness Rangers.*
Provides:
Training, barracks housing, some positions offer a stipend. Two winter positions for interpretive naturalists provide government housing, training, uniform, and subsistence for up to $15 a day.

California - Passport in Time

Address: PIT Clearinghouse, PO Box 18364, Washington, DC 20036
Phone: 202-293-0922
Fax: 202-293-1782
Contact: Jill Shaefer

Passport in Time offers free vacations helping on historic preservation projects in California.

Two prehistoric archaeological sites—a rock shelter that has been looted, and a village site severely eroded by Mill Creek—will be excavated in the Ishi Wilderness. For 4,000 years, this region was the Yahi Indian homeland with several Yahi villages in the canyons. Volunteers will map sites, process artifacts and stabilize the sites before they are lost.

Two Civilian Conservation Corps projects need repair. The Dow Butte Lookout, constructed in 1939, is using volunteers to restore the interior and exterior of the structure as an interpretive stop for visitors. Later it will be moved to the shore of Eagle Lake to be integrated into a trail network.

The McCarthy Point Fire Detection Lookout structure, built by the Civilian Conservation Corps in 1936, is a unique one-story building. Volunteers will help restore the exterior of the lookout, which will be used as an interpretive site.

Volunteers are also welcome in Mendocino National Forest to restore an 1860 log cabin. In Shasta-Trinity National Forest, you can replace the shake roof and windows and paint the Forest Glen Guard Station, built in 1916.

In Tahoe National Forest, you search for artifacts in way stations along the Henness Pass Road, used by early gold and silver seekers before the railroad was built.

Cost:
   FREE.
Number of programs:
   6
Age range:
   18 and over, or 16-17 if accompanied by adult.
Children:
   No.
Major emphasis:
   Historic preservation.
Sample programs:
   Archaeology assistants to map site. **Carpenters and roofers** to repair building. **History enthusiasts** to look for mining artifacts.
Provides:
   Varies. Campsites, equipment, instruction, materials.

California - Sequoia & Kings Canyon National Parks

Address: Three Rivers, CA 93271
Phone: 209-565-3341
Contact: Volunteer Coordinator

Cost:
FREE.
Number of programs:
Several.
Age range:
Over 18.
Children:
No.
Major emphasis:
Parks preservation.
Sample programs:
Field work with water quality. *Trail maintenance*, backcountry. *Campground hosts*.
Provides:
Uniforms. Free campsite for campground hosts, and possible reimbursement for utilities. For 32 hours a week, housing may be available. Backcountry trail workers may get meals or a small stipend. Additional stipends may be available.

John Muir decribed Kings Canyon as "a rival to the Yosemite." Cedar Grove lies in this glaciated valley of the Kings River, and from the highway, travelers see towering granite cliffs, tumbling waterfalls, and a powerful river. The Cedar Grove area is an entrypoint to hundreds of miles of spectacular wilderness trails for hikers or horseriders only.

"We welcome volunteers, but they should realize that we expect them to work while they are here," says Jan Blackshire, volunteer coordinator. "People sometimes don't realize that we need to get things done."

The Grant Grove area of Kings Canyon National Park leads to magnificent giant sequoia trees, waterfalls, miles of secluded trails, and superb vistas. Created in 1890 to protect the sequoias from being cut down, it contains the General Grant Tree, the third largest living tree in the world. The Giant Forest of Sequoia National Park also has many outstanding sequoias soaring over 200 feet. To the west are dry foothills with oak trees and vegetation that stretches down to the San Joaquin Valley.

Volunteers are needed year-round and part-time for a variety of positions. You can help with lab and field work on acid rain, water quality, and sequoia research. You can lead hikes and walks and school-related activities. You can maintain backcountry trails, serve as a campground host, or help with computer programs and administration. Because of cutbacks in funding for paid staff, there may be more opportunities for volunteers.

Canoe Country Escapes

Address: 194 South Franklin Street, Denver, CO 80209
Phone: 303-722-6482
Contact: Brooke & Eric Durland

Paddling a canoe along the peaceful waterways between Lake Superior and the Canadian Rockies takes you across thousands of interconnected lakes, streams and waterfalls known as the Minnesota-Ontario Boundary Waters. It's a unique way to explore wilderness areas. It's the specialty of this company, in business for almost 20 years. You hear loons calling across the lake, watch evening sunsets sink into the forest, and have time for swimming, fishing, and bird-watching.

You can take one of three lodge-to-lodge canoeing routes and stay in comfortable lodge and pre-set campsites where the cook prepares meals before your arrival. Wilderness Medleys are all-camping canoe trips. Family Trips avoid hard paddling and offer a layover every other day. Children five and up are welcome and usually enjoy discovering mushrooms, moose droppings, and frogs!

"We find that the layover day is often the favorite of the trip," note the Durlands, a husband-and-wife team. "That's when you can fish your heart out, pick blueberries, swim to that island across from your campsite, or catch some sun."

The company also offers custom trips, and rents equipment and a planned route for a do-it-yourself wilderness experience.

Cost:
From $302 to $1,652
Number of programs:
About 24.
Age range:
12 and up.
Children:
Yes. Age 12 and under, reduced rates.
Major emphasis:
Canoe trips in the Minnesota-Ontario Boundary Waters.
Sample programs:
Lodge-to-Lodge Canoeing, 6 days, $895. ***Family Trips***, cabin/camping, 3 days, $595. ***Custom Guided Trips***, 6 people, 3 days, $302.
Provides:
Accommodations, all meals, guides, canoe instruction and practice session, life vests, equipment, transportation, free airport pick-up in Duluth.

Canyonlands Field Institute

Address: PO Box 68, 1320 So. Highway 191, Moab, UT 84532
Phone: 800-860-5262: 801-259-7750
Fax: 801-259-2335
Contact: Jon Orris or Tim Severns

You can walk along Anasazi Indian trails, look for lizards, paddle in cool mountain lakes, and explore the high plateaus of Colorado and Utah with Canyonlands Field Institute.

A non-profit educational organization, CFI has promoted stewardship of the Colorado Plateau region through outdoor education programs for students of all ages since 1984. Programs are held in the canyons of the Green and Colorado rivers, Arches and Canyonlands national parks, the La Sal Mountains and the Navajo and Hopi Reservations.

CFI's Outdoor Science School offer a two- to six-day river experience for youngsters in grades 4 to 12, or a three- or five-day stay in a yurt near Moab, Utah, to explore wilderness areas. Elderhostel programs offer river trips, including intergenerational programs for grandparents and grandchildren to enjoy floating together down the San Juan River to learn about the wildlife, plants, prehistoric rock art and geology.

Summer Day Camp and weekend programs explore desert wildflowers, lizards, archaeology, and river ecology. A Desert Writers Workshop is held at a historic ranch. Courses for professional guides include Red Cross emergency response and river rescue techniques. Custom trips for families or groups can be arranged.

Cost:
CFI membership, $20 individual. Nonprofit organization. Prices from $75 to $500. Scholarships are available to qualified individuals who can influence others to promote an environmental ethic.

Number of programs:
3 a month year-round.

Age range:
5 to 80.

Children:
Best age is 6 to 15.

Major emphasis:
Natural/cultural history, sciences, low-impact recreation and camping.

Sample programs:
Rocks & Minerals of Moab, 2 days, $75. *Elderhostel Intergenerational River Trip*, 5 days, $360. *Outdoor Science School*, grades 4 to 12, 6 days, $420.

Provides:
Accommodations (varies with program), guides, equipment, instructions, all meals (varies with program), transportation.

"I liked the part about orienteering and the camouflage game. I think it's neat how we can learn about science without studying a book. It was loads of fun." 3rd grader from Utah

Caretta Turtle Research Project

Address: Savannah Science Museum, 4405 Paulsen Street, Savannah, GA 31405
Phone: 912-355-6705
Contact: Todd Gedamke, Director

The Caretta Turtle Research Project is a hands-on research and conservation program on the beaches of Wassaw National Wildlife Refuge near Savannah, Georgia, to save the loggerhead sea turtle, known by its Latin name, *Caretta*. The project began in 1973. Its goals are:

√ to learn more about population levels, trends and habits of the loggerhead turtle;
√ to help eggs and hatchlings survive on a nesting beach;
√ to get members of the public involved in the work.

The project operates under a cooperative agreement with the US Fish and Wildlife Service, which administers the refuge.

Volunteers travel to the island for one-week sessions from mid-May through early October every year. Working in small groups with a leader, they move and protect nests, monitor the nests after the eggs are laid, and later escort the newly-born turtles to the surf. During the day, they check and maintain numbered beach markers, inspect nests for predators or storm damage, dig up and record contents of hatched nests, and survey the beaches for dead turtles.

A staff expert explained: "During egg-laying, you will spend most of each night patrolling Wassaw Island's six miles of beaches, searching for the huge female loggerheads as they crawl out of the surf to nest. You and your research team will tag each turtle, take measurements of the turtle and its path to the nest, and record other important information."

You should be able to walk a few miles along a beach at night, using natural light, not a flashlight. Experience has shown that cheerful, upbeat, and adaptable people cope best under the crowded conditions (participants live in two small cabins), and with insects, rain storms, heat, and humidity. So far, more than 1,700 volunteers have taken part in the project.

Cost:
$475 for a week.
Number of programs:
One a week, May to October.
Age range:
18 and over.
Children:
No.
Major emphasis:
Turtle preservation.
Sample programs:
One week working on beaches to protect turtles.
Provides:
Accommodations, all meals, training, transportation, van from the Savannah Science Museum to island and back.

Colorado Dude & Guest Ranch Association

Address: PO Box 300, Tabernash, CO 80478
Phone: 303-887-3218
Contact: Wright Catlow

Imagine a Western ranch vacation where you ride your horse on tree-shaded trails and through soaring red rock canyons with a cool breeze gently blowing. You can enjoy such an experience for free if you offer to work at the ranch and they need volunteer help. Or you pay for a week's stay, and enjoy the relaxed pace of Western life, still an affordable vacation because everything's included.

CDGRA members represent 40 ranches in Colorado that have been personally inspected to ensure they meet the Association's standards. Some ranches are high up in the Colorado Rockies with snow-covered mountain peaks within hiking distance, while others nestle in the sheltered valleys near the foothills where temperatures soar to over 90 degrees on hot days. Some are working ranches run by families and you are welcomed as their guest. Others are full-time resort ranches that no longer raise cattle but keep horses for guests.

You may stay in a picturesque lodge, with all modern amenities, a cabin complete with bathroom, or share a three-bedroom log cabin with friends or family. Meals are always home-cooked and fresh, and special diets are respected. You'll get a cowboy-size breakfast, a light lunch or packed lunch if you're out for the day, and a delicious family-style dinner, with plenty of fresh vegetables and fruit.

There's always an extensive horseriding program. You may be assigned your own horse for the week, or just take rides on different horses each day, or join rides a couple of times to admire the spectacular scenery. Daily activities may include hiking or rafting, a hay ride, square dancing, cookouts and campfires, fishing, or gold panning. Or you can mellow out in a heated pool or spend the day in a rocking chair on the porch.

Cost:
From $830 to $1,500 per week. Can volunteer to work at ranch.
Number of programs:
40 members of CDGRA. Some open year-round.
Age range:
All ages.
Children:
Welcome at any age.
Major emphasis:
Western ranch activities.
Sample programs:
Harmel's Ranch Resort, Almont, 150 guests, one week, $830. **Focus Ranch**, Slater, 30 guests, one week, $950. **Wind River Ranch**, Estes Park, 56 guests, one week, $1125. **C Lazy U Ranch**, Granby, 115 guests, one week, $1500.
Provides:
Accommodations, all meals, activities, guides, instruction, equipment, entertainment, pre-trip information, transportation.

Colorado - Mesa Verde National Park

Address: PO Box 8, Mesa Verde National Park CO 81330
Phone: 303-529-4475
Contact: Sarah Craighead

Located in the southwest corner of Colorado, Mesa Verde National Park is a World Heritage site. Its archaeological remains are astonishing to modern eyes. At some time between AD 1190 and 1300, the Anasazi built huge cliff houses, with more than 100 rooms, some four stories high. After the Anasazi disappeared, the Ute Indians came to the Mesa Verde area, and avoided the cliff dwellings. The Spanish explorers never saw them, and it was not until 1888 that two ranchers discovered the Cliff Palace, one of the largest sites, with more than 200 rooms and 23 kivas.

Mesa Verde was declared a National Park in 1906 after many artifacts had been taken by visitors over the years, and was the first park set aside exclusively for its archaeological significance.

Today, volunteers are welcome year-round to help with natural resource work, visitor interpretation, administration and maintenance.

Cost:
FREE.
Number of programs:
Several
Age range:
Over 18.
Children:
No.
Major emphasis:
Service projects.
Sample programs:
Maintenance Assistant. Visitor Center and Interpretation.
Provides:
Small subsistence may be available. Housing may be available in spring, fall, winter.

Colorado - South Park Ranger District

Address: USDA Forest Service, Pike & San Isabel National Forests, PO Box 219, Fairplay, CO 80440
Phone: 719-836-2031
Contact: Sharon Kyhl

Cost:
FREE.
Number of programs:
Several
Age range:
Over 18.
Children:
No.
Major emphasis:
Service projects.
Sample programs:
Mountain Bike Trail Coordinator. Forest Interpreters. Wilderness Rangers.
Provides:
Limited bunkhouse quarters available. Most positions need valid driver's license.

Within easy reach of Denver, this beautiful area includes Lost Creek and Buffalo Peaks Wilderness and stretches for an estimated 465,000 acres. With more territory over 9,000 feet than any other Colorado county, it contains the high plateaus of the region, flat grassy plains surrounded by spectacular mountain peaks over 13,000 feet and inhabited by elk, bighorn sheep, deer and mountain goats. There are the remains of hundreds of 19th-century structures left by the miners and settlers who once lived and worked in the area.

Volunteers are welcome from mid-May to mid-September, and some positions include weekends. If you volunteer for more than two weeks, you may receive a stipend of $60 for 40 hours of work a week. A one-month commitment is required, and you are welcome to stay longer, or for the whole season. Training and orientation are given in June, or whenever new volunteers arrive.

Positions available include interpreters to serve at a visitor center and develop interpretive campground and special programs; wilderness rangers to check campsites, educate visitors on low impact techniques, and do light trail maintenance; trail crew members to maintain trails; and biological aides to help with research. Coordinators are needed to organize volunteer trail groups, and instruct in methods of trail construction. Mountain bike trail coordinators inventory all mountain bike rides. Wilderness rangers need to be in good shape to hike wilderness and backcountry trails and monitor use.

Colorado State Parks Volunteers

Address: 1313 Sherman Street, Room 618, Denver, CO 80203
Phone: 303-866-3437
Fax: 303-866-3206
Contact: Laurie Mathews, Director

Cost:
FREE.
Number of programs:
24 state parks.
Age range:
18 and over.
Children:
With families.
Major emphasis:
Volunteer work outdoors.
Sample trips:
Off-Season Watchman, Jackson Lake State Park, Orchard, 6 months. *Campground Host*, Eleven Mile State Park, Lake George, 3 weeks minimum. *Park Naturalist*, Lathrop State Park, Walsenberg, May 31-Labor Day.
Provides:
Campsite, training, supervision.

For a free vacation in any of Colorado's state parks, you can volunteer to be a campground host, lead nature walks, or work on trail maintenance work, among other options. While some parks need only one or two people each year, others can employ 20 or more. A few positions provide training, while others require a driving license and no criminal record. Just complete an application form, and send it to the location where you want to volunteer.

Steamboat Lake and Pearl Lake state parks need four campground hosts, and provide a campsite per couple. Ridgway State Park needs five campground hosts, two boat patrol rangers, two park naturalists, two trail construction crew leaders and about 25 trail workers. Campsites with full hookups are usually provided free of charge.

Cherry Creek State Park in Aurora has campsites for eight volunteer campground hosts. Golden Gate Canyon State Park needs two couples to serve as park hosts and backcountry volunteers to work on different projects, and provides campsites if needed.

"Volunteers have made a significant contribution to Colorado state parks, "We are fortunate that people are interested in helping maintain and protect Colorado's natural heritage."
Laurie Mathews, Director

Colorado Trail Foundation

Address: 548 Pine Song Trail, Golden, CO 80401
Phone: 303-526-0809
Contact: Gudy Gaskill

The dream of walking across Colorado has become a reality since Gudy Gaskill started to organize and co-ordinate thousands of volunteers to create the Colorado Trail in 1974. Today, she is president of the Colorado Trail Foundation, and hundreds of hikers, bikers, and horse-riders enjoy the breath-taking views along the trail. The 500-mile route crosses eight mountain ranges, seven national forests, six wilderness areas, and five river systems.

Most of the trail is above 10,000 feet and many areas are above 12,000 feet, with the highest point being 13,334 feet so you see wildflowers, alpine tundra, and snow-covered peaks. Walking the entire trail takes about six to eight weeks, and requires careful planning.

Every summer, volunteer work crews help to keep the trail in good condition. Weekend crews are out on Saturdays and Sundays. Week-long crews get to the rendezvous point on Saturdays, then drive or hike to base camp and set up tents. Sunday, a free day, usually provides an introduction to trail techniques and safety measures. The crews work four days and have Wednesday free, though there's an optional group hike. Friday evening there's a farewell dinner and awards ceremony.

A crew leader is in charge and assigns food preparation, wood collecting and other chores. Each crew member packs lunch in the morning, and walks to the site.

Cost:
FREE. Non-profit organization. $35 one-time registration fee.
Number of programs:
15 to 25, summer only.
Age range:
16 to 90.
Children:
Welcome but not encouraged.
Major emphasis:
Repair and relocate trail tread.
Sample programs:
Trail crews. Trail maintenance. Adopt-A-Trail Program.
Provides:
Accommodations, all meals, equipment including hard hat and tools, instruction, pre-trip information.

"I've been going for seven or eight years, and for the past two years I've been in charge of getting all the food for the trail crews. It's a great experience for all ages."
Special education school assistant, Parker, Colorado

Country Inns Along the Trail

Address: RR #3, Box 3115, Brandon, VT 05733
Phone: 802-247-3300
Fax: 802-247-6851
Contact: Director

You spend your days skiing in the fresh air in winter, and hiking or biking in summer along clearly marked trails in Vermont's Green Mountains. You relax in the evenings and overnight at delightful country inns with sumptuous meals and a hot shower. It's a unique adventure escape.

The ski touring follows the Catamount Trail, which runs the length of Vermont's Green Moutains, with stays at three different inns. The tour is self-guided and is recommended for experienced skiers. You can also ski on trails near each inn.

In spring, summer, and fall, you can hike Green Mountain trails under shady green trees with occasional views. Your host will take you to the trailhead after you leave your car at the trail's end, enabling you to drive to the next inn. Bike tours take you along charming country roads from inn to inn.

Cost:
About $100 per person per day.
Number of programs:
About 12.
Age range:
All ages.
Children:
Yes.
Major emphasis:
Inn-to-inn ski, hike, or bike tours.
Sample programs:
Catamount Excursion Ski Tour, 4 days, $459.
Provides:
Accommodations, all meals, taxes, gratuities, shuttle for point-to-point skiing or hiking.

"I had a wonderful time on this trip. For me, it was an ideal combination for outdoor activity, physical exercise, informal socializing, and fine dining."

Participant on ski tour

Country Walkers

Address: PO Box 180, Waterbury, VT 05676-0180
Phone: 800-464-9255: 802-244-1387
Fax: 802-244-5661
Contact: Bob & Cindy Maynard

Now in their 17th year of running quality vacations in the outdoors, Bob and Cindy Maynard offer walking tours led by qualified guides in Vermont, Maine, California, Arizona, Washington, and also in Canada, Europe, New Zealand, Costa Rica, and Chile. Groups of no more than 20 participants walk through scenic countryside and interesting towns. You stay in country inns or hotels. The pace is comfortable, and walkers cover between four and 12 miles a day. A van transports the luggage from inn to inn.

The Pacific Northwest walk begins in Seattle with a van ride to the Olympic Peninsula. Hikes include the Enchanted Valley Trail, a beach walk at Kalaloch, the Hoh River Trail, Hurricane Ridge Trail, and an easy walk to Marymere Falls. In Arizona's Sonoran Desert, you hike Wasson Peak in the Tucson Mountains, where spring wildflowers and saguaro cacti grow and where you may see desert birds, Sabino Canyon in the Santa Catalina Mountains, visit the Arizona Sonora Desert Museum, and walk along the San Pedro River.

In Maine's Acadia National Park, you can admire the dramatic rocky coastline; hike Blue Hill Mountain, Cadillac Mountain, and Eagle Lake; and visit the historic town of Castine. The central Vermont tour begins in Stowe, with walks along Trapp Family Lodge trails, on the Mt. Mansfield Alpine Tundra Walk, through old farming communities, and on the Long Trail to Lake Pleiad, a pristine alpine lake.

Cost:
From $725 to $3,395.
Number of programs:
More than 100.
Age range:
Most people are between 35 and 70.
Children:
No.
Major emphasis:
Quality walking adventures.
Sample trips:
Central Vermont, 5 days, $789. *Sonoran Desert*, SE Arizona, 7 days, $1,499. *Coast of Maine*, 5 days, $825.
Provides:
Accommodations, most meals, excursions, guides, entry fees, tips, pre-trip material, support vehicle, transportation.

"The whales frolicking in front of us during our first day's picnic was really a special treat."
Participant from Massachusetts, Nova Scotia Walk

"This is my fourth walking vacation with you and they have all been A+!"
Participant from Connecticut, Olympic Peninsula Walk

Craftsbury Running Camps

Address: **Craftsbury Sports Center, Craftsbury Commons, VT 05827**
Phone: **800-729-7751: 802-586-7767**
Fax: **802-586-7768**
Contact: **Director**

Runners of all levels enjoy a unique experience in northeast Vermont at this 140-acre sports facility. Expert coaches, nationally ranked runner/instructors, quiet roads, good food, and interesting classes help runners and triathletes improve their performance levels.

The day begins with a coached group run, ranging from a walk-jog to six-minute-per-mile speeds, followed by stretching and videotape of runners' strides. After breakfast, there are classroom seminars on mental training, nutrition, sports medicine, and physiology. After that there are cross-training sessions in swimming, biking, deep water running, or sculling.

Lunch is served at 12:30, followed by free time to sunbathe or enjoy a massage, or take a horseback or bike ride. In the afternoon, an optional road or track workout is offered. After dinner, activities include volleyball, campfire, or dancing.

For guests at the center, there's swimming, canoeing, or tennis courts available at any time. They can also rent mountain bikes, scull boats or horses to ride by the hour. Special weeks focus on triathletes and over-40 runners, and participants can enter local races.

Cost:
From $420 to $535.
Number of programs:
About 6 every summer.
Age range:
Any age. Average camp age: 36.
Children:
Babysitting can be arranged.
Major emphasis:
Running and multi-sports programs.
Sample programs:
Run-Marathon Training Camp, 6 days, $495. *Run-Multisport Camp*, 6 days, $495. *Run Camp & Stowe Road Race*, 7 days, $535.
Provides:
Accommodations, all meals, instruction, equipment, activities, T-shirt.

Crater of Diamonds State Park

Address: Route 1, Box 364, Murfreesboro, AR 71958
Phone: 800-628-8725: 501-285-3113
Contact: Park Ranger

Cost:
    $4 adult, $1.50 child.
    Campsite: $14.50 a day.
Number of programs:
    One.
Age range:
    Any age.
Children:
    Welcome.
Major emphasis:
    Hunting for diamonds.
Sample programs:
    Mine entrance fee, $4 daily fee.
Provides:
    60 campsites with water and electriticy. Rental digging equipment available.

Diamond-hunting on vacation could change your life. Imagine discovering a million-dollar gem lying in the ground! Well, it's a fantasy, but the diamond hunting part is for real.

In Arkansas, you can walk in a 35-acre field—which is the eroded surface of an ancient gem-bearing volcanic pipe—where real diamonds have been found. It's the only diamond site where anyone can prospect for and keep gems found. You enter the field through the park visitor center, which includes exhibits and a program explaining the area's geology as well as tips on recognizing diamonds in the rough. Digging tools are available for rent, and the park staff provides free identification and certification of diamonds.

Diamonds were first discovered in the field in 1906. Since then over 70,000 have been found, including a 40.23-carat, a 16.37-carat, and a 15.33-carat called the "Star of Arkansas." After the area became a state park in 1972, over 17,000 diamonds have been carried home by visitors. You can also find other precious gems: amethyst, garnet, jasper, agate, quartz and more.

Every year there's an annual Diamond Exposition where famous diamonds found at the Crater are on display in the park visitor center.

Crow Canyon Archaeological Center

Address: 23390 Country Road K, Cortez, CO 81321
Phone: 800-422-8975
Fax: 303-565-4859
Contact: Lynn Dyer/Director Marketing

Archaeologists at Crow Canyon Archaeological Center are conducting important long-term research focused on the events leading up to the final abandonment of the Mesa Verde region by the ancestral Puebloan Anasazi people by the year 1300. They welcome interested students and adults to assist them with work at the excavation sites and in the laboratory.

"There is no need for previous experience in archaeology," explains Lynn Dyer, "Every year, hundreds of novices, ranging from young adults to retirees, participate in our research."

The excavation programs run from mid-May to mid-October. Participants work for a week or longer. Crow Canyon also offers year-round programs that explore the richness of Native American culture and the grandeur of this remote yet magnificent landscape, where Native Americans have lived for over a thousand years.

Researchers hope to explain why the ancestral Puebloan people living on and around the Mesa Verde Plateau in southwestern Colorado disappeared. They left behind no written accounts of their complex culture, which had flourished for more than a thousand years, except for deserted communities built of stone, filled with the items of daily life.

Cost:
From $795 to $2,700.
Number of programs:
Several.
Age range:
All ages.
Children:
Special programs and above.
Fourth grade and above.
Major emphasis:
Archaeology.
Sample programs:
Archaeology Program, one week, $795. *Exploration & Seminar Programs*, $895-$2,700.
Provides:
Accommodations, meals, tuition, training, equipment.

Desert Survivors

Address: PO Box 20991, Oakland, CA 94620-0991
Phone: 510-357-6585
Contact: Steve Tabor, President

Cost:
FREE trips for members. Membership: $20. Nonprofit organization.

Number of programs:
About 50 a year.

Age range:
Mostly 25 to 55.

Children:
Over 9 welcome with parent.

Major emphasis:
Desert natural history and adventure.

Sample programs:
Death Valley & Joshua Tree National Parks, car-camping. Backpacking, climbing, hiking trips in California and Nevada. Weekends and week-long trips of varying difficulty.

Provides:
Guides, instruction, pre-trip material, trip reunions.

Desert Survivors, founded in 1978 by two friends, is a growing group of people who enjoy exploring the Western desert wilderness and are committed to its study and protection. Trips range from weeks-long rigorous backpacks to weekend car-camping and day hiking. Some hikes to explore lava flows, lava tubes, and cinder cones in Lava Beds National Monument in California; other hikes include a swim in a hot pool in the Anza-Borrego Desert State Park; or there's a trip to the largest known Joshua tree in the Joshua Tree National Park. You can also hike to Mono Lake and Panum Crater.

Members of Desert Survivors also work to keep the region wild, and provide comments on desert preservation issues. They often appeal Bureau of Land Management decisions on development, monitor potentially harmful activity proposed within the seven million acres of BLM Wilderness Study Areas in the California desert. They also publish *The Survivor*, a quarterly journal.

"Our hikes are an essential link to the protection effort," notes president Steve Tabor. "Hikers become familiar with the areas proposed for both wilderness and development, and collect data on such topics as the extent of desert tortoise and bighorn sheep habitat, and the range of off-road vehicles incursions into sensitive areas."

"The sunset valleys swimming in a pink and lilac haze, the great mesas and plateaus fading into blue distance, the gorges and canyons banked full of purple shadow...the desolation and the silence of the desert." John Charles Van Dyke, The Desert

Dinamation International Society

Address: 550 Crossroads Court, Fruita, CO 81521
Phone: 800-DIG-DINO
Fax: 303-858-3532
Contact: Jonathan Cooley

You're on your knees in dirt, digging away carefully with a small trowel and scooping up the earth when suddenly you see a lump in the dirt. You stop, and grab a brush to clean it off. Holding your breath, you see the outline of a small bone. It's part of a dinosaur backbone that has been lying in the earth for millions of years. Your leader is exultant, the bone position is carefully recorded, and your discovery is photographed before going off to the laboratory.

It's a high point on a dinosaur dig. For would-be paleontologists, this is an ideal adventure vacation. Previous participants have made significant finds, including the world's largest and oldest known Apatosaurus, the oldest known Armored Dinosaur in North America, and a nesting site of the small Dryosaurus. All the programs are led by expert paleontologists who instruct participants on exactly what to do. You'll stay at a nearby hotel or motel, and drive to dig sites during the day.

You'll also enjoy excursions to state parks and places of interest, such as the Canyon Science and Learning Center near the main entrance to Colorado National Monument in Fruita which displays lifelike robot dinosaurs and has a demonstration classroom.

Colorado, Utah, Arizona, and Wyoming are the centers of dinosaur research in the United States. If you don't want to dig, you can take a tour of the different sites. In addition, international dinosaur expeditions take you to Mexico, Argentina, England, and Indonesia.

Cost:
From $775 to $1,250.
Number of programs:
12
Age range:
Ages 6 and up.
Children:
Best age is 6 to 12.
Major emphasis:
Dinosaur dig expeditions.
Sample programs:
Family Dino Camp, Colorado Canyons, 5 days, $775. *Dinosaur Diamond Safari*, 6 days touring, $850. *Wyoming High Plains*, 6 days, $1,050.
Provides:
Accommodations, excursions, guides, equipment, instruction, pre-trip material, most meals, transportation.

"This is a wonderful chance for family members to learn about dinosaurs together." 		Father on dig with his two sons

Dirt Camp for Mountain Bikers

Address: 3131 Endicott Drive, Boulder, CO 80303
Phone: 303-499-3178
Fax: 303-494-5826
Contact: Rod Kramer

Mountain bikers can ride with and learn from world class professionals at experiential mountain bike training camps held in Colorado and Utah, and in Chamonix, France. The week-long Dirt Camps offer coaching and training techniques, nutritional information, and great riding opportunities with the experts.

Staff members include Skip Hamilton, world class endurance athlete and coach for many elite racers, and Andy Pruitt, one of the foremost medical authorities on cycling, as well as top professional racers.

In spring and fall, there's a Dirt Camp in Moab, Utah, which offer rides along fantastic mountain trails. In summer, the Dirt Camp is high in the Rockies in Crested Butte, Colorado, where you follow mountain trails through a sea of wildflowers. The Dirt Camp for bikers is followed by Crested Butte Medical Camp.

Each Dirt Camp accepts up to 30 participants, divided into small groups according to ability. Ride difficulty and length will be matched to each group, and most rides are 3 to 6 hours long. Van support is available for each individual ride. You can test bikes from the fleet of demo machines and try out new accessories and equipment. Plan on bringing your own bike.

Campers stay in comfortable hotels with a swimming pool, hot tub, and a large bike mechanic room. Meals are designed for active cyclists, with low-fat and carbo-loading menus.

Cost:
$850.

Number of programs:
4 in USA, 1 in France.

Age range:
16 and over.

Children:
13 and over. 17 and younger must be accompanied by an adult.

Major emphasis:
Mountain biking.

Sample trips:
Spring Moab Camp, 7 days, $850.
Crested Butte Ride, Colorado, 7 days, $850.

Provides:
Accommodations, all meals, equipment, instruction, transportation.

ALSO:
Ask about the company's tandem bike tours for 8 or more riders in California, Colorado, and France.

"Thank you again for making Dirt Camp so terrific. Everything turned out even better than my wildest expectations!"
Participant from New York

Earthwatch

Address: 680 Mt. Auburn Street, Watertown, MA 02272
Phone: 617-926-8200
Fax: 617-926-8532
Contact: Blue Magruder

Cost:
From $795 to $1,795. Non-profit organization.
Some fellowships available.
Number of programs:
155.
Age range:
16 to 80.
Children:
16 and over.
Major emphasis:
Environmental research.
Sample programs:
Tracking Timber Wolves, Minnesota, one week, $795. *Big Bend Volcanoes*, Texas, 10 days, $1,195. *Rocky Mountain Wildflowers*, Colorado, 2 weeks, $1,495.
Provides:
Accommodations, all meals, instruction, hand-out materials, transportation.
Volunteers make a contribution to Earthwatch for programs and pay their own travel.

Since 1972, Earthwatch and EarthCorps volunteers have assisted environmental research projects around the world. The Center for Field Research receives hundreds of proposals from scientists who need help. Earthwatch provides the people to work with the scientists. Through firsthand experiences, volunteers understand the significance of research efforts to preserve the environment. More than 4,000 men and women aged 16 to 80 have participated.

In the United States there are some 35 projects. At South Dakota's aptly named Mammoth Graveyard, you can help paleontologists dig up incredible Columbian mammoths. The animals died at the site more than 26,000 years ago, and so far fossils of 50 mammoths as well as remains of the first wolf and the giant short-faced bear have been found.

In Aptos, California, Evelyn Hanggi wants to show that horses are capable of understanding abstract relationships, and is assaying the learning abilities of three horses. You stay in a farmhouse on a horse facility, and help set up and perform the tests.

Many coral reefs worldwide are slowly eroding from silt-laden runoff. Off the coast of Maui in Hawaii, certified divers and marine experts are attempting to document the status of pristine or near-pristine reefs to form a baseline. You make two dives daily, setting up transects, identifying fish along them, surveying coral species, and measuring water quality.

In Wisconsin, where the call of the loon across a peaceful lake is a sound that echoes in the memory, you can help researchers in their fourth season examining previously color-marked loons to determine the effects mercury has on certain behaviors.

"With its warm closeness and friendly involvement between people of diverse nationalities, ages, education, and experience, Earthwatch is probably unique." 90-year-old participant

Florida - Everglades National Park

Address: 40001 State Road 9336, Homestead, FL 33034-6733
Phone: 305-242-7700, Ext. 7254
Contact: Volunteer Coordinator

It looks like a sea of grass at first glance, but this unusual park hides a variety of animals and wildlife if you take time to slow down and explore. You may see alligators, waterbirds, ducks, turtles, otter, and deer. The Florida panther, black bear, and bobcat were residents at one time, but are rarely sighted today. The park has been declared a World Heritage Site and an International Biosphere Reserve. It covers more than 2,000 square miles.

More than 250 people volunteer each year at Everglades National Park. Most positions are available from November to April, but some are open year-round. You can work in an office, do maintenance, clean up beaches and trails, help with biology and hydrology data collection, remove exotic plants, assist with environmental education, and answer questions at visitor centers. Uniform shirts and hats are provided, and there's an awards banquet at the end of March.

Most volunteers stay at campgrounds near by because housing and trailer sites are extremely limited. If you volunteer in the summer months, a house or trailer site can be arranged, but the park staff know that the "mosquito meter" often reads "unbearable" during this time of year. Because it's a popular park, there are often several applicants for each opening, so apply early.

Cost:
FREE.
Number of programs:
Several.
Age range:
Over 18.
Children:
No.
Major emphasis:
Park preservation and maintenance.
Sample programs:
Assist research on native plant inventory. ***Maintain trails***. ***Lead interpretive programs***.
Provides:
Training, uniforms, chance to explore park. Limited housing. No stipends.

Florida State Parks

Address: **Marjory Stoneman Douglas Building,**
              3900 Commonwealth Boulevard, Tallahassee, FL 32399
Phone: **904-488-8243**
Contact: **Philip A. Werndli**

Volunteers are welcome to help in more than 100 Florida state parks, of which 42 have campsites. You can request application forms and a free guide to the parks describing the different parks. Contact the parks directly. You can volunteer for a few hours a week, a few days, a month, or more.

There are a range of positions: You can assist at information centers, present living history programs, do building maintenance, work in a park library, take photographs, lead nature walks, assist at campgrounds, clear trails, demonstrate art and craft skills, help with special events, collect litter, and assist with environmental research.

The parks vary greatly. The Homosassa Springs State Wildlife Park is home to the gentle manatee, as well as crocodiles and alligators. Boat tours are provided daily, and there's an Animal Encounters Area to see snakes and other native wildlife.

Bulow Plantation Ruins Site was once a prosperous plantation of sugar cane, cotton, rice and indigo, and was destroyed in the Second Seminole Indian War. Today visitors follow a trail to the sugar mill for a history of the plantation.

Cayo Costa State Park is on a barrier reef island and its miles of beaches, acres of pine forest, oak palm hammocks, mangrove swamps and a spectacular display of birds can be reached only by boat or the public ferry.

Cost:
   FREE.
Number of programs:
   In 100 parks.
Age range:
   Over 18.
Children:
   Accompanied by parents.
Major emphasis:
   Park preservation and maintenance.
Sample programs:
   Campground Hosts. Nature Walk Leaders. Artists and Craftspeople
   for demonstrations.
Provides:
   Orientation, training, campsite, trailer hook-up.

Glacier Institute

Address: PO Box 7457, Kalispell, MT 59904
Phone: 406-756-3911
Contact: Kris Bruninga

Education about the environment of Glacier National Park is the focus of this institute, founded in 1983 by Dr. Lex Blood. The programs are held at two field sites: the Glacier Park Field Camp, and the Big Creek Outdoor Education Center.

Seminars and field trips explore the wildlife and wild flowers of the region. An intensive introductory course on grizzly bears studies bear habitat, mythology, management, and the problems of bear/people conflicts. Bring binoculars, though the chances of seeing a bear are slim.

Other programs include children's *Saturday Naturalists* courses, youth programs, college-level seminars, Elderhostel programs, and ecology field camps.

Cost:
$20 to $550. Non-profit organization.
Number of programs:
About 50.
Age range:
6 to senior citizens.
Children:
Best age from 9 to 18.
Major emphasis:
Environmental education in Glacier National Park area.
Sample programs:
Glacier's Grizzlies, 16 and older, 2 days, $130. *Youth Camp*, ages 9 to 18, 6 to 8 days, $250 to $325. *High Country Adventures*, 18 and older, 7 days, $550.
Provides:
Accommodations, all meals, instruction, hand-out materials, transportation.

Gold Vacations - Colorado

Address: Phoenix Gold Mine, PO Box 3236, Idaho Springs, CO 80452
Phone: 303-567-0422

A vacation looking for gold in a gold mine may be not only free, but profitable! In the Colorado mining community of Idaho Springs, a half-hour drive from Denver, there's a working underground mine where real miners still push tons of gold and silver ore in small rail cars just as they did a century ago. Visitors take a tour and may dig their own rich gold ore sample. In spring and summer visitors can also pan for gold along the stream.

Since its discovery in 1871, the Phoenix and related veins have produced more than $2 million in gold and silver. After periods of activity, the mine was virtually shut down until 1972 when it was acquired by the present owners. In 1974, the owner's 14-year-old son—now a mining engineer and son of a third generation Colorado miner—made a promising surface discovery of a rich gold vein. The mine has been in operation ever since.

Most of Colorado's formerly profitable gold and silver mines are now abandoned, or open only as tourist attractions. Gold was first discovered in Denver's Cherry Creek in 1858, and by 1859 prospectors had reached the rich placer gold deposits in what is now Idaho Springs. This discovery sparked the Pike's Peak Gold Rush, rivaled in size only by the 1849 California rush and the Klondike rush of 1897.

The Idaho Springs-Central City area districts had the largest production of any comparable area in the Front Range Mineral Belt. Since 1859, the Colorado Mineral Belt has produced more than $12 billion of gold and silver.

Cost:
    $6.00 adults, $3.00 children.
Number of programs:
    One.
Age range:
    All ages.
Children:
    Welcome.
Major emphasis:
    Seeing a working underground silver and gold mine.
Sample programs:
    Tours from 10 a.m. to 6 p.m. daily.
Provides:
    Tour guides, parking.

Gold Vacations - Georgia

Address: Dahlonega Welcome Center,
101 S. Park Street, Dahlonega, GA 30533
Phone: 800-231-5543 ext. 10: 706-864-3711

Dahlonega was the center of the nation's first gold rush in 1828 in the Georgia Mountains, one hour's drive north of Atlanta. In the Courthouse Gold Museum, you can see an exhibit commemorating the event, and the 23-year operation of a branch of the US Mint. There are still working mines where you can pan for gold and look for precious gems.

ALSO Consolidated Mines, offers tours and gold panning. 706-864-8473.
Crisson's Gold Mine and Camp, offers gold panning. 706-864-6373.
Blackburn Park has camping, swimming and gold panning. 706-864-4050.

Cost:
Varies.
Number of programs:
Several.
Age range:
All ages.
Children:
Welcome.
Major emphasis:
Working gold mine, gem hunting, and gold panning.
Sample programs:
Tours and camping.
Provides:
Tour guides, facilities, parking.

Hawaii - Haleakala National Park

Address: PO Box 369, Makawao, Maui, HI 96768
Phone: 808-572-9306
Contact: Pamela Rasfeld

Haleakala, the House of the Sun, is the world's largest dormant volcano. It covers about 33 square miles, is seven miles long, two miles wide, and 21 miles in circumference. Visitors can hike along 30 miles of well-marked trails, including across the floor of the crater. Here you find a wasteland reminiscent of the moon's landscape, with cinder cones, lava flows, and mountains of sand and rock.

One of the most spectacular sights is to arrive before dawn and watch the sun rise. The legend says that it was at Haleakala that the god Maui lassoed the sun to slow its track across the sky so that his mother had more daylight to dry her "tapa" cloth.

Volunteers are welcome year-round but must make a commitment for three months. There are only a few positions available. These include interpreters, who provide visitor information and lead walks; resource managers to monitor endangered plant species; and maintenance workers to rebuild and preserve the trails. To apply for research projects such as monitoring eco-systems, you need a science degree.

Cost:
    FREE.
Number of programs:
    Several.
Age range:
    Over 18.
Children:
    No.
Major emphasis:
    Preservation, maintenance, research.
Sample programs:
    Interpreters to give talks and lead walks. *Maintenance workers* to build and keep up trails. *Research Assistants* to monitor for science projects.
Provides:
    Housing, possible small stipend.

Hostelling International/American Youth Hostels

Address: 733 15th Street NW, #840, Washington, DC 20005
Phone: 800-444-6111: 202-783-6161
Fax: 202-783-6171
E-mail: dkalter@attmail.com (for Discovery Tours)
Contact: Toby Pyle

Cost:
Membership fees: $25 adult, $10 under 18, $15 over 54. Non-profit organization. Prices range from a few dollars to $30 overnight.

Number of programs:
Almost 5,000 hostels worldwide.

Age range:
All ages.

Children:
Welcome.

Major emphasis:
Bargain accommodations and affordable tours.

Sample programs:
Overnight fees: ***Teepee on Vashon Island***, Seattle, $9. ***Lighthouse Hostel***, California, $11. ***Historic building***, New York City, $22 summer, $20 winter.

Provides:
Accommodations, kitchen facilities, information, activities, programs.

Imagine staying in Hawaii, minutes from Waikiki Beach, for $15 a night. Or how about a ski vacation right by the slopes in Winter Park, Colorado, for $12.50 a night?

You can do it if you stay at HI-AYH hostels. These are low-cost dormitory-style lodgings where you share a communal kitchen, and can meet other travelers. Hostelling International directories list nearly 5,000 hostels in over 70 countries. You can join the organization no matter what your age—the word "youth" refers to your spirit. Founded in 1934, there are more than 125,000 HI-AYH members throughout the United States.

In the US and Canada directory, you'll find hostels in almost every state and province, including Alaska. There are 38 HI-AYH Regional Offices, and reservations services at hostels in Washington, Boston, Los Angeles, New York City, Ottawa, Seattle, and nearly 100 other North American hostels. You can reserve a bed in many hostels around the world up to six months in advance with the toll-free 800 number.

Every hostel is individual. On the California coast, there are two hostels in historic lighthouses. In New York, you stay in a landmark historic Manhattan building. On Vashon Island near Seattle, you can stay in a log cabin, covered wagon, or one of five Sioux Indian tepees. In Ohio, there's a hostel on a 900-acre working farm.

HI-AYH Discovery Tours offer about 30 low-cost one- to three-week summer bike, hike, backpack, camping, and van trips for groups ranging from teens to seniors.

Idaho - Panhandle National Forest

Address: 1201 Ironwood Drive, Coeur d'Alene, ID 83814
Phone: 208-765-7230
Contact: Shirley M. Hooper

Panhandle National Forest covers almost 2.5 million acres in five counties of northern Idaho. There are three lakes, mountain hiking trails, remote campsites, snowmobile trails in winter, backcountry roads, and rivers and streams for canoeing and rafting. You'll find plenty of openings for volunteers and about 600 people a year perform services in the park.

You can help on a trail crew or timber crew, act as maintenance worker, caretaker, or campground host, or work on projects with professional biologists, hydrologists, geologists and others. Call for details about different projects and tell them if you have any special talents.

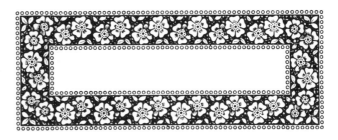

Cost:
FREE.
Number of programs:
Many.
Age range:
Over 18.
Children:
No.
Major emphasis:
Preservation, maintenance, research.
Sample programs:
Trail Crew Workers to clear trails.
Campground/Picnic Ground Hosts.
Research Assistants to work with professionals.
Provides:
Depends on project.

"We treat our volunteers as special people. We want them to enjoy their work and our beautiful area."   A staff member

Idaho - Passport in Time

Address: PIT Clearinghouse, PO Box 18364, Washington DC 20036
Phone: 202-293-0922
Fax: 202-293-1782
Contact: Jill Shaefer

Passport in Time invites volunteers to enjoy free vacations helping on a variety of historic preservation projects in Idaho. You can help archaeologists excavate a site on Bartoo Island in Idaho Panhandle National Forest as a basis for nominating the site for the National Register of Historic Places.

Curlew National Grasslands in southern Idaho, in Caribou National Forest, was home to prehistoric people who roamed the region. Volunteers work with a crew of university archaeological students to test-excavate a large site to help determine its age.

The interconnecting mountains of the Bitterroot Range in Clearwater National Forest served as a migration route for thousands of years. The Lewis and Clark expedition came to the Nez Perce territory in 1805 along this route, and Chief Joseph and his non-treaty Nez Perce traveled over the same route in 1877 while fleeing General Howard's troops. Volunteers work on a systematic inventory to identify, record, and protect historic, prehistoric and cultural values of the trail.

In Salmon National Forest, volunteers float the Salmon River in rafts and stop at strategic locations to inventory the shoreline for signs of Native American hunters and hermits who once lived along the river.

Other projects include test excavations in Boise National Forest; continuing excavation of a gold prospector's campsite dating to the 1890s; restoring the 1927 Sourdough Peak Lookout in Nez Perce National Forest; and archaeological testing and evaluation of a 5,000-year-old fish midden in Wallowa-Whitman National Forest.

Cost:
    FREE
Number of programs:
    9 in Idaho.
Age range:
    18 and over.
Children:
    No.
Major emphasis:
    Historic preservation.
Sample programs:
    Archaeology assistants. Historical researchers.
Provides:
    Campsites, trailer hook-ups, free lodging in college dorms.

Indiana - Wayne National Forest

Address: USDA Forest Service, 608 West Commerce, Brownstown, IN 47220
Phone: 812-358-2675; 812-275-5987
Contact: Larry Mullins

Stretching 188,000 acres across the hills of southern Indiana, and surrounded by people eager to use its outdoor recreation facilities, Wayne National Forest, the only designated wilderness in Indiana, faces the problem of being overused and overrun with visitors.

Volunteers are needed as maintenance workers on hiking trails and as campground hosts for 300 camp units and 100 miles of trails. Researchers can assist on environmental projects and work with geologists, hydrologists, cave experts, biologists, paleontologists, and archaeologists. There's also a need for artists to provide murals, skits and plays as well as original music, painting and photographs for visitor programs to teach appreciation of the natural environment.

Active horse-riders with their own horses are needed to ride along trails and distribute information, do light maintenance and serve as hosts at horse camp.

Cost:
FREE.
Number of programs:
Several.
Age range:
Over 18.
Children:
No.
Major emphasis:
Preservation, maintenance, research.
Sample programs:
Wilderness Equestrian Hosts with own horse. *Artists* to create murals, write music, skits and plays. *Researchers* to assist on environmental projects.
Provides:
Depends on project. Free camping, some mileage, some daily subsistence stipends.

International Wolf Center

Address: Vermilion Community College, Environmental Studies, 1900 E. Camp Street, Ely, MN 55731
Phone: 800-657-3609
Fax; 218-365-7207
Contact: Program Coordinator

You ride out to wolf pack territories in northern Minnesota and howl like a wolf in hope of getting a response. This is one of the programs offered by the International Wolf Center at Vermilion Community College. IWC's mission is to act as a focal point for worldwide environmental education about wolves, and support the survival of the wolf by teaching about the animal's life, its interrelationships with other species, and its role within human cultures.

At the Center, you can observe young wolves who have been raised in captivity from the age of 10 days as they chase each other, bite, and play with a stick in their enclosure. On Winter Wolf Weekend programs, participants ski, snowshoe, and dogsled through Superior National Forest, looking for the signs of wolves and other animals. From a plane, the group tries to spot a wolf pack in the snow-covered Great Lakes region.

A dogsledding adventure takes you out to watch veteran mushers and wilderness instructors demonstrate how to dog sled, and then you mush your own dog team in the frozen landscape. Other programs show how to build snow shelters, demonstrate winter wilderness skills, and explain wolf ecology. A program hosted by the Ojibwe Indians, who have always had a special relationship with the wolf, Ma'ingan, includes sacred legends and pipe and drum ceremonies.

Cost:
$55 to $585. Non-profit.
Number of programs:
About 15.
Age range:
18 and over.
Children:
Welcome at family programs.
Major emphasis:
Education about wolves.
Sample programs:
Winter Wolf Weekends, 3 days, $335.00. *Winter Wilderness Seminar*, 4 days, $460.00. *Wolf Research Expeditions*, 5 days, $585.00
Provides:
Accommodations, all meals, equipment, instruction, pre-trip material, transportation.

"I had no idea that I would learn as much as I did about wolves or try so many new things: cross-country skiing, dogsledding, small plane ride."   Participant on Wolf Weekend

"This is a great opportunity for people, especially those of us from the south who wouldn't have these experiences normally."
Participant from North Carolina

Massachusetts Audubon Society

Address: 208 South Great Road, Lincoln, MA 01773
Phone: 800-289-9504
Fax: 617-259-8899
Contact: Tricia Hamilton or Sue Moody

Cost:
$1,050 to $5,495.
Number of programs:
25 a year.
Age range:
45 to 80.
Children:
Not recommended. Some voyages suitable for 10 and over.
Major emphasis:
General natural history with birding slant.
Sample programs:
Big Bend, Texas, 9 days, $1,075. *Everglades National Park & Dry Tortugas*, 8 days, $1,325. *Alaska, Cruising the Inside Passage*, 8 days, $3,980.
Provides:
Accommodations, all meals, excursions, naturalist guides, transportation, entry fees, tips, taxes, reading lists.

Birdwatching, nature walks, and natural history are emphasized on trips to southern California, Alaska, Texas, Arizona, Baja California and other places in North America, as well as abroad to Costa Rica, the Galapagos islands, Belize, New Zealand, and Africa. The society's excursions are all led by naturalists and biologists.

"These are not trips for late risers or those requiring luxurious accommodations" warns the introduction to one tour. MAS travelers rise at dawn for early morning hikes to spot birds, who are always up earlier. In Arizona, you visit Santa Catalina State Park before breakfast, and then travel to Saguaro National Monument to birdwatch in the desert. There are also visits to a sanctuary where gray hawks and vermilion flycatchers make their nests.

In Florida's Everglades, you look for wading birds including the tricolored heron, reddish egret, white ibis and roseate spoonbill. From Key West, you take a boat to explore the Dry Tortugas National Park, and look for nesting seabirds such as the sooty tern and brown noddy.

The Florida Gulf Coast trip visits the National Audubon Society's Corkscrew Swamp Sanctuary, which boasts the largest remaining stand of virgin bald cypress, and Sanibel Island and the Ding Darling National Wildlife Refuge, which shelters alligators as well as many shore birds.

Michigan - Isle Royale National Park

Address: 800 E. Lakeshore Drive, Houghton, MI 49931-1895
Phone: 906-487-9081: 906-482-0986
Contact: Intern Program

Cost:
FREE.
Number of programs:
Several internships.
Age range:
Over 18.
Children:
No.
Major emphasis:
Service projects.
Sample programs:
Photography Intern. Natural Resource Intern. Backcountry Campground Host.
Provides:
Dormitory accommodations, travel to island, uniform allowance, $70 weekly stipend.

On Lake Superior, almost on the Canadian border, is a wilderness park that is truly isolated. Isle Royale is an island 45 miles long and 9 miles wide, with hiking trails and camping facilities, and a string of lakes ideal for exploring on a boat. Wildlife abounds and you may see moose, fox, and a wide variety of birds and waterfowl. There's backpacking and fishing available, and plenty of time to kick back on the shore.

A volunteer intern program for the summer offers several positions for people with skills. The photography intern helps operate the park darkroom and maintain the park historic photo collection, as well as take, develop, print and enlarge photos. The natural resources intern assists in monitoring water, air, and acid rain; monitoring and counting bald eagle, osprey, and loons; compiling backcountry permit data; monitoring airplane flights; and assisting with a variety of field research efforts.

The Resource Center Intern helps with the interpretive program, and is responsible for the park library. The Backcountry Campground Host lives and works in a remote backcountry campground assisting the ranger with maintenance, patrols and other duties.

Training for interns starts May 30. Interns are expected to make a 12-week commitment, 40 hours a week. Since there's some travel through the area, camping, backpacking and small boat experience is desirable. Volunteers share two-person dorm rooms at island headquarters, and cook in a communal kitchen. Free travel to the island from Houghton, Michigan, is provided on a government-owned vessel.

Other volunteer positions are available through the Student Conservation Association.

"Enthusiasm is an important qualification!" Staff member

Michigan - Passport in Time

Address: Clearinghouse, PO Box 18364, Washington, DC 20036
Phone: 202-293-0922
Fax: 202-293-1782
Contact: Kathleen Schamel

Passport in Time invites volunteers to enjoy free vacations helping on a variety of historic preservation projects in Michigan.

The Manistee and Au Sable rivers in Huron-Manistee National Forest were well-known highways across northern Michigan before roads were built. Though little is known of those who lived along the rivers or traveled down them, volunteers will survey the Au Sable River and its tributaries, and assist with mapping.

Prehistoric people hunted, fished, and gathered berries in this region from 8000 BC to 1000 AD along Hagerman Lake in Ottawa National Forest. Today, volunteers will map the site, and wash and catalog artifacts that include pottery and stone tools.

Before California's Gold Rush, there was an 1840s Copper Rush in Michigan, and the greatest mining boom began about 1850. The Norwich Copper Mine, an example of the exploration, speculation, and development of copper, is a well-preserved complex of four mine locations around two towns with mills, cabins, boarding houses, stores, and a church. Volunteers will continue to map mine features, and help with artifact collecting, washing, and cataloging.

Cost:
  FREE.
Number of programs:
  3 in Michigan.
Age range:
  18 and over.
Children:
  Over 16 with adult.
Sample programs:
  Survey Assistants along river.
  Excavation Assistants on lake.
Provides:
  Varies. Campsites, camping.

Minnesota - Voyageurs National Park

Address: PO Box 50, International Fall, MN 56649
Phone: 218-283-9821
Contact: Ron Meer

Water dominates the Voyageurs National Park landscape, set in northern Minnesota near the Canadian border. You'll find more than 30 lakes—some huge, some small—within its boundaries. Between the lakes are bogs, marshes and beaver ponds. The only way to explore is by boat, just as the early fur traders and explorers did in the 18th and 19th centuries.

Moose, bear, and deer live in the region, and it is also home to the rare eastern timber wolf, who hunts the deer. Osprey, eagle, and great blue heron nest in the park. You may see kingfishers, mergansers, loons and cormorants. You can boat from island to island, camp on beaches, hike on nature trails, and fish for northern pike, lake trout, and perch. In winter, there's skiing and snowshoeing along the trails, and icefishing in the lakes.

Volunteers with biology experience can help with research into fish habitat where you sample fish in park lakes, and record and compile data. There are also openings for assistants for research projects on large mammals in the region, and at visitor centers.

Cost:
   FREE.
Number of programs:
   Several.
Age range:
   Over 18.
Children:
   No.
Major emphasis:
   Service projects.
Sample programs:
   Aquatic Research Aides. Naturalists for canoe trips and nature walks. *Trail Maintenance* assistants.
Provides:
   Housing, $8 a day stipend.

Montana - Little Bighorn Battlefield National Monument

Address: PO Box 39, Exit 510 I-90 Hwy 212, Crow Agency, MT 59022
Phone: 406-638-2621
Contact: John Doerner

This historic battle site marks the tremendous victory of the combined forces of Lakota, Cheyenne, and Arapaho warriors against Lt. Col. George Custer and five companies of the Seventh Cavalry. The battle lasted for two days, June 25 and 26, 1876.

Volunteers are needed to present interpretive programs to visitors, and to assist the museum curator and chief historian with the museum collections and library. Qualifications are a knowledge of American frontier history, computer systems, and the Library of Congress Catalog system. You should enjoy meeting people, be able to speak in public and work on your own. If you stay 30 days or more, a one-bedroom efficiency apartment is provided.

Cost:
FREE.
Number of programs:
One.
Age range:
Over 18.
Children:
No.
Major emphasis:
History.
Sample programs:
Presenter for interpretive programs.
Assistant for historical research.
Provides:
Apartment for 30 days or more.

ALSO:
Bureau of Land Management is responsible for more than 8.4 million acres of public land in Montana, North Dakota, and South Dakota. Volunteers welcome as campground hosts, recreation assistants, nature trail maintenance, museum assistants, and other positions.
Contact:
BLM/Montana State Office,
222 N. 32nd Street, Billings MT 59107
Phone: 406-255-2827

Montana - Passport in Time

Address: Clearinghouse, PO Box 18364, Washington, DC 20036
Phone: 202-293-0922
Fax: 202-293-1782
Contact: Kathleen Schamel

Passport in Time invites volunteers to enjoy free vacations helping on a variety of historic preservation projects in Montana.

In Beaverhead National Forest, the Canyon Creek Charcoal Kilns were associated with the Hecla Consolidated Mining Company, one of Montana's most successful silver and lead mining businesses. The site has 22 large brick kilns built in the 1880s to make charcoal for use in smelters in nearby Glendale, now a ghost town. Volunteers work with a master brick mason to restore the kilns.

The Monument Ridge quarry, located along the crest of the Gravelly Mountains at 9,559 feet, has revealed remains of toolmaking areas and campsites left by ancient hunters in southwestern Montana. Previous volunteers surveyed 2,000 acres and recorded 12 new prehistoric sites dating from 6500 BC.

Other archaeological programs include excavations at the Bowman Spring Site in Helena National Forest, the Cabinet Mountain Wilderness Survey in Kootenai National Forest, excavations of prehistoric encampments probably 3000-1000 BC in Deep Creek Park, and walking surveys, site recording and mapping at the Gibson Reservoir site in Lewis & Clark National Forest.

In Flathead National Forest, volunteers help restore three old log structures along the Spotted Bear River next to the Bob Marshall Wilderness, and in Lolo National Forest, help is needed to finish the reconstruction of the Hogback Homestead, a hand-hewn log cabin built in 1917.

Cost:
FREE.
Number of programs:
8 in Montana.
Age range:
18 and over.
Children:
Over 16 on some projects.
Sample programs:
Assist rebuilding old homesteads. Assist anthropology and archaeology research.
Provides:
Campsites, camping, RVs.

Mountain Travel-Sobek

Address: 6420 Fairmount Avenue, El Cerrito, CA 94530-3606
Phone: 800-227-2384: 510-527-8100
Fax: 510-525-7710
Contact: Liz Longstreth

An experienced adventure company, Mountain Travel-Sobek was created in 1991 when two travel companies merged. Today, you can join their adventurous trips around the world, from Antarctica to Vietnam, from China to Costa Rica, from Africa to Australia. Their elegantly produced full-color catalog is an adventure traveler's dream book.

In the United States, travel with them to Alaska and the Arctic region for rafting, hiking and exploration in the wilderness. Visit the Arctic National Wildlife Refuge and float on the Sheenjek and Kongakut Rivers, with hikes to explore the region and look for mountain sheep, wolves, grizzly bears, and a variety of birds. Late June, when summer begins, the caribou return to their summer range and plants burst into flower for the short blooming season. By August, the tundra and cottonwood groves are ablaze in spectacular red and yellow.

On the Alsek River raft trip, you take a helicopter to bypass Turnback Canyon, and at night there are spectacular views of the northern lights.

Special accredited programs in wilderness medicine, mountain medicine, international health and travel medicine are offered. Seminars in Wilderness Medicine are held in Alaska, Chile, Tanzania, Switzerland, Brazil, Bolivia, Baja, New Guinea, Spain, and Baja California. Topics covered include high-altitude illnesses, hypothermia, wilderness trauma, dehydration, common parasitic infections, and traveler's diarrhea.

Cost:
From $1,000 to $4,000.
Number of programs:
Over 100.
Age range:
30 to 55.
Children:
Depends on trip.
Major emphasis:
Adventure travel around the world.
Sample programs:
Arctic National Wildlife Refuge, rafting/hiking, 12 days, $1,850. *Alsek River, Alaska,* rafting/hiking, 12 days, $1,995. *Wilderness Medicine Seminar,* rafting/hiking, 11 days, $3,810.
Provides:
Accommodations, most meals, excursions, guides, equipment, instruction, pre-trip material, transportation on land.

"I truly feel that the trip was excellent in every aspect. It was definitely one of the most impressive and positive experiences of my life to date." Participant on Alsek River

National Audubon Society

Address: 700 Broadway, New York, NY 10003
Phone: 212-979-3067
Fax: 212-353-0190
Contact: Margaret M. Carnwright

Cost:
$1,090 to $7,990
Number of programs:
About 10.
Age range:
Adults.
Children:
Depends on program.
Major emphasis:
Environmental nature travel.
Sample programs:
Canyons of Time, 8 days, $1,855.
Alaska's Coastal Wilderness, 8 days,
$3,980. *Iceland, Greenland &
Hudson Bay,* 16 days, $7,990.
Provides:
Accommodations, all meals, instruction, pre-trip material, guides, excursions.

National Audubon tours are led by staff experts and focus on birds, plants, animals, wildlife sanctuaries, and nature refuges around the world. The Society has sponsored travel programs for its members since the 1940s, and you can join for $20 and take any tour.

In North America, you can explore Alaska's Coastal Wilderness, looking for humpback whales just off Point Adolphus, watching glaciers calve into the water, and passing harbor seals basking on ice floes. In Alaska, join the Tatshenshini River Wilderness Rafting expedition. A week-long *Canyons of Time* tour explores Bryce, Zion and Grand Canyon National Parks, where you hike the trails of Zion Gorge, home to more than 250 species of birds; tour the five-mile rim of Cedar Breaks National Monument with its spectacular natural amphitheater; and explore the Grand Canyon's North Rim.

The Society drafted *The National Audubon Society Travel Ethic for Environmentally Responsible Travel* to provide rules for tour operators, leaders, and travelers, reprinted in full at the end of the book. Key points are:

1. Wildlife and their habitats must not be disturbed.

2. Audubon tourism to natural areas will be sustainable.

3. Waste disposal must have neither environmental nor aesthetic impact.

4. The experience a tourist gains in traveling with Audubon must enrich his or her appreciation of nature, conservation, and the environment.

5. Audubon tours must strengthen the conservation effort and enhance the natural integrity of places visited.

6. Traffic in products that threaten wildlife and plant populations must not occur.

7. The sensibilities of other cultures must be respected.

National Wildlife Federation

Address: 1400 16th Street NW, Washington, DC 20036-2266
Phone: 800-245-5484: 703-790-4363
Fax: 703-790-4468
Contact: Barbara Mayritsch

The National Wildlife Federation offers outdoor adventures for kids, teens, adults, educators and families. Its popular one-week summer Conservation Summits take place in different states near beautiful natural scenery.

A variety of classroom and outdoor activities allow adults and families to explore each region and design their own schedules as they choose from classes and field trips on ecology, bird watching, nature photography, and geology. About six weeks before the Summit, participants receive a handbook detailing the adult courses offered, so they can decide which courses to take.

At each Summit there are classes for educators, focusing on nature study teaching techniques, integrating environmental education into an existing curriculum, and other environmental education materials.

NWF, one of the largest environmental groups in the country, is composed of affiliate organizations in nearly every state and territory, and also has Associate Members around the country. It also offers award-winning Wildlife Camps for youth aged 8-13, and Teen Adventure Programs for young people aged 14-17, in Colorado and North Carolina; NatureQuest workshops and special training for camp program directors, nature and science counselors, naturalists and outdoor educators; and travel expeditions abroad.

Cost:
$680 to $6,290. Membership $22. Non-profit organization.

Number of programs:
3 Summits a year. 9 travel programs abroad.

Age range:
Preschoolers to seniors.

Children:
Welcome from 3 to 17.

Major emphasis:
Nature study, outdoor recreation.

Sample programs:
Colorado Rockies Conservation Summit, Estes Park, one week, $680. *Hawaii Conservation Summit*, Hilo, one week, $680. *Alaska Odyssey*, 8 days, $2,505.

Price includes:
Accommodations, all meals, recreational facilities, excursions, instruction, guides.

Natural Habitat

Address: 2945 Central Green Court South, Boulder, CO 80301
Phone: 800-543-8917: 303-449-3711
Fax: 303-449-3712
Contact: Lee-Ann McKenzie

Cost:
$1,395 to $5,700.
Number of programs:
20.
Age range:
All ages.
Children:
No.
Major emphasis:
Animal-watching eco-tourism.
Sample programs:
Seal Watch, Magdalen Islands, Canada, 5 days, $1,695. *Polar Bear Watch,* Churchill, Canada, 8 days, $1,995. *Brown Bear Watch*, Katmai, Alaska, 13 days, $3,995.
Provides:
Accommodations, airfare on trip, pre-trip materials, naturalist guides, some meals, instruction, lectures, activities, excursions, equipment.

Fluffy newborn seal pups crawl on the floating icefields as you stroll among thousands of mother seals with their snow-white babies. Once threatened with extinction, a 1987 Canadian ban on commercial hunting has saved the seals, and Natural Habitat works with other organizations to ensure that tourism and minimal hunting can help them survive.

Ben Bressler, the company's founder, says: "As people become more aware of the importance of endangered wildlife and the environment, they are becoming more interested in witnessing these incredible animals. We began with one destination and now we take travelers to watch animals in 22 different areas around the world."

The company arranges tours in Alaska to watch brown bears fishing for salmon just a few feet away. There's a wildlife expedition to see orca and humpback whales, sea lions, seals, puffins, and bald eagles, as well as a bear flightseeing tour. In Churchill, Canada, you look for polar bears on the tundra, and may see Arctic foxes and snowy owls as well. In a Quebec conservation park, you track wolves.

The company offers animal-watching trips in Australia, Zimbabwe, Costa Rica, and Antarctica, among others. Research Adventures allow you to help scientists working with wolves, Azores whales, dolphins, and polar bears.

Many tours provide overnight accommodations in hotels and inns, and are designed as "soft" adventure trips. "We want to make it easy for people of all ages and abilities to experience the splendors of the animal kingdom," says Bressler.

"My trip to the harp seals was an absolute dream come true. To pet a baby harp seal was the greatest thrill of my life."
Participant from Arizona on **Seal Watch**

Nature Expeditions International

Address: PO Box 11496, Eugene, OR 97440
Phone: 800-869-0639: 503-484-6529
Fax: 503-484-6531
Contact: Trip Director

Adventure, learning and discovery programs in North America, Central America, South America, Asia, Africa, and Oceania are the specialty of NEI, founded in 1973. Expert leaders take small groups off the beaten track to explore the natural and cultural environment. All leaders are required to have a masters degree, Ph. D., or the equivalent, and college-level teaching experience in their appropriate field. Leaders include top biologists, anthropologists, natural history and outdoor education specialists.

In Alaska, you explore Glacier Bay and Kenai and Denali national parks, home to grizzly bears, moose, Dall sheep, whales, birds, and wildflowers, and there's a cruise in the Gulf of Alaska and the Inside Passage.

In New Mexico and Arizona, you visit archaeological centers at Chaco Canyon, Mesa Verde, and Bandelier, as well as the Grand Canyon and Monument Valley, led by Natalie Pattison, currently photo archivist for the University of New Mexico's Museum of Anthropology where she teaches Southwestern prehistory and ethnology.

In Hawaii, you can take a natural history tour of different islands and look for seals, dolphins, whales and exotic fish as well as learn about Hawaiian culture.

Cost:
From $1,390 to $5,200.
Number of programs:
38.
Age range:
25 to 75.
Children:
12 and older welcome.
Major emphasis:
Wildlife, natural history, and culture.
Sample programs:
Southwest Indian Country, 8 days, $1,390. *Hawaii Natural History*, 15 days, $2,490. *Gulf of Alaska & Inside Passage*, 11 days, $3,500 to $5,200.
Provides:
Accommodations, most meals, excursions, guides, equipment, instruction, pre-trip material, transportation on land.

New Mexico - Carlsbad Caverns National Park

Address: 3225 National Parks Highway, Carlsbad, NM 88220
Phone: 505-785-2232
Contact: Volunteer Coordinator

Caves! If you love the idea of going down under the earth and exploring the rocky pathways inside caves, this may be the ideal vacation for you. Volunteers are welcome to help on a variety of projects, but you should have some interest in caves, the desert, or dealing with the public. Volunteers can also apply through the Student Conservation Association Resource Assistant Program, listed later in this section of the book.

Carlsbad Caverns in southeastern New Mexico is part of a national park that covers 47,000 acres of the Chihuahuan Desert. So far, more than 80 caves have been discovered, and new discoveries are constantly being made. During the day, visitors take tours of the caves to see the incredible formations.

Among the marvels to be seen are Giant Dome, the biggest 62-foot-high stalagmite; the Iceberg Rock, a 100,000-ton boulder that fell from the ceiling thousands of years ago; the 42-foot high Twin Dome in the Hall of Giants; and numerous other stalactites and stalagmites. At dusk, watch thousands of Mexican free-tail bats fly from the cave for a night of feasting on insects.

Cost:
FREE.
Number of programs:
Several.
Age range:
Over 18.
Children:
No.
Major emphasis:
Caves and desert.
Sample programs:
Interpretive presentations. Maintenance assistants.
Provides:
Housing and trailer spaces with hookups may be available, and possible stipend of up to $5 a day.

ALSO:
Bureau of Land Management, Albuquerque District and Taos Resource Area, welcomes volunteer campground hosts and trail technicians. Free campsites or trailer, with a small allowance for food.
Contact:
BLM/Taos Resource Area,
224 Cruz Alto Road, Taos NM 87571
Phone: 505-758-8851
Contact: John Bailey.

New Mexico - Passport in Time

Address: Clearinghouse, PO Box 18364, Washington, DC 20036
Phone: 202-293-0922
Fax: 202-293-1782
Contact: Kathleen Schamel

Passport in Time invites volunteers to enjoy free vacations helping on a variety of historic preservation projects in New Mexico.

In Gila National Forest, you can learn basic archaeological methods as you work with experts at Apache Creek Ruin. Here, the Mogollon Indians once lived on the banks of the Tularosa River, between AD 1100 and 1250. Volunteers will excavate, stabilize, and curate artifacts.

Projects in Santa Fe National Forest include the repair of a 1930s stucco and adobe structure featured in *The Milagro Beanfield War*; work on the interior of reconstructed Gallina house; documenting rock art at Glorieta Mesa; and excavating and mapping a Spanish village dating back to 1760. Also, there are numerous prehistoric cliff dwellings at Sapillo Creek, and volunteers assist in recording the dwellings, pictographs, and raw material quarry.

Volunteers record and document the remains of Cooney/ Claremont, two historic mining towns in west central New Mexico, using mapping and photography.

In Carson National Forest at Pot Creek Cultural Site, the ancestral home of both the Taos and Picuris Pueblos, volunteers, assisted by Native Americans will reconstruct a pueblo and pithouse. In Lincoln National Forest, volunteers will excavate a two- or three-room structure dating from AD 1200, which is being damaged by erosion.

You can research and write materials on the history of the Rio Chama area for the education program at Gateway to the Past Museum at Ghost Ranch Living Museum. And volunteers are needed for the reconstruction of Borracho Cabin, built at the turn of the century, and used by Forest Service personnel until the 1920s.

Cost:
FREE.
Number of programs:
11 in New Mexico.
Age range:
18 and over.
Children:
Over 8 allowed on some projects with an adult.
Major emphasis:
Historic preservation.
Sample programs:
Archaeology assistants. Mapping and surveying assistants. Writers.
Provides:
Campsites, camping, Rvs, depending on program.

North Carolina - Blue Ridge Parkway

Address: 200 BB & T Building, One Pack Square, Asheville, NC 28801
Phone: 704-271-4779
Contact: VIP Coordinator

The Volunteers in Parks program welcomes people to help at visitor centers, demonstrate old time crafts such as weaving and spinning, play traditional music, help maintain trails, post boundaries, and assist with clerical and administrative work.

Many enjoy the Campground Host program. For a period of one to six months, you live on a free site in one of the Parkway's nine campgrounds, give information to campers about the region, and help Park Rangers register and orient campers. When funds are available, you get a modest reimbursement for out-of-pocket expenses (usually $5 per day for lunch) and for travel mileage from your local residence to the Parkway.

The Blue Ridge Parkway winds for 469 miles along the crests of the Southern Appalachian mountains amid the forested slopes of North Carolina and Virginia. The road links two national parks—Shenandoah National Park and Great Smoky National Park. The scenic drive presents a magnificent panorama of views, forests, mountains and trees, though it is sometimes hidden in misty clouds. In the spring there are hundreds of azalea, laurel, and rhododendron in bloom, and you can see wildflowers throughout the summer.

Cost:
FREE.
Number of programs:
Many.
Age range:
Over 18.
Children:
No.
Major emphasis:
Preservation and upkeep of recreation sites.
Sample programs:
Campground Hosts. Maintenance assistants.
Provides:
Campsite. Possible meal and mileage reimbursement.

North Cascades Institute

Address: 2105 Highway 20, Sedro Woolley, WA 98284
Phone: 206-856-5700 ext.209
Fax: 206-856-1934
Contact: Kirsten Tain

Outdoor seminars that take participants into the beautiful scenery of Washington's North Cascades region are the specialty of the Institute. Participants go hiking to Swakane Canyon to observe butterflies, backpack to the Pasayten Wilderness to read poetry and prose amid the mountains, and hike to the Lake Chelan-Sawtooth Wilderness Area to look for plants and wildflowers. Others programs cover nature writing, raptors, rocks, minerals and fossils, marine mammals, meteorology, amphibians, and birds.

"Our small, informal classes bring together eager learners and gifted teachers in nature's classroom," notes Saul Weisberg, Executive Director and an Institute founder. "We spend full days in the field—listening and learning from the voices of the land. Each evening we gather for one of our famous potlucks to share good food and camaraderie."

You can choose from a wide variety of year-round courses related to the region as well as Elderhostel programs, teacher training, conferences, and Mountain School, Mountain Camp, and Skagit Watershed Projects for children.

Cost:
From $55 to $715.
Number of programs:
More than 50.
Age range:
All ages.
Children:
Welcome on most programs.
Sample programs:
Family Seashore Adventure, weekend, $55. ***Butterflies of the South Cascades***, weekend, $275. ***Mountain, River, Sea,*** rafting/sailing, 7 days, $715.
Provides:
Varies. Can include accommodations, meals, camping, instructors, and sometimes transportation. Call for details of individual programs. Scholarship fund available for youth programs and low-income participants.

"I learned that a watershed isn't just water, it's the mountains and the things that are surrounding the water. We have to take care of the land and the water together."
Fourth-grade student, Skagit watershed project

Ohio Department of Natural Resources

Address: **Ohio DNR, Divn. of Wildlife,**
                1840 Belcher Drive, Bldg. G-1, Columbus, OH 43224
Phone: **614-265-6372**
Contact: **Phil King**

A wide range of environmental volunteers are needed for more than 100 wildlife areas around the state of Ohio. The Division of Wildlife also operates five district offices, research stations, fish hatcheries, a pheasant production facility, visitor centers, and shooting ranges.

Volunteers can help survey wildlife, round up geese, count birds, and monitor nest boxes and eagles' nests. Other openings include planting trees and maintaining bluebird trails and butterfly gardens. You can also make educational presentations at schools and meetings, and lead tours of wildlife areas and fish hatcheries.

Cost:
    FREE.
Number of programs:
    Many.
Age range:
    Over 18.
Children:
    No.
Major emphasis:
    Wildlife preservation and survey.
Sample programs:
    Wildlife Research assistants. *Attendant* at shooting range. *Presenter* to groups.
Provides:
    Depends on project.

Olympic Park Institute

Address: 111 Barnes Point Road, Port Angeles, WA 98362
Phone: 206-928-3720
Fax: 206-928-3046
Contact: Office

You can boat in the San Juan Islands in search of sea mammals. You can take a wilderness coast backpack along rugged and pristine beaches. Try a weekend studying butterflies or the geography of the Olympic Mountains, or the Ancient Rainforests of the Hoh. You can take a wildflower painting class along the shores of Lake Crescent or join a family Seashore Safari.

Olympic Park Institute programs encourage hands-on education and firsthand experiences in the park. The region is a mixture of rainforests and tree farms, glaciated mountains and wildflower meadows, aquatic habitats, fish hatcheries, and cultural resources.

Many seminars are held at the Rosemary Inn and run from Friday evening to Sunday afternoon. There are also off-campus hiking and backpacking programs. Groups are small and informal. "We balance the elements of having fun to inspire learning," notes a staff member.

The Olympic Park Institute, founded in 1984, is located on scenic Lake Crescent in the Olympic National Park, and is dedicated to preserving the natural beauties of the region through outdoor adventure programs. One of three campuses operated by the Yosemite National Institute, OPI received the 1989 Environmental Award of Excellence.

Cost:
 $15 to $325.
Number of programs:
 60.
Age range:
 2 to 80.
Children:
 Welcome at some classes.
Major emphasis:
 Outdoor education and adventure, natural history, science, the arts.
Sample programs:
 Seashore Safari for families, one day, $16. *Elk & Mammals of Olympic National Park*, 2 days, $79. *Alpine & Old Growth Photography*, weekend, $169. *Wilderness Coast Backpack*, 5 days, $169.
Provides:
 Accommodations, all meals, excursions, professional naturalists, instruction.

"A great place to learn about our environment and ourselves in a stunningly beautiful place surrounded by extraordinary individuals. Only thing I didn't like: leaving to return home."
Participant from Washington.

"It was challenging and I learned a lot. The parts I enjoyed the most were the wild animals and learning about the animals and plants." Participant on Young People's Backpack

Oregon - Deschutes National Forest

Address: Crescent Ranger District, PO Box 208, Crescent, OR 97733
Phone: 503-433-2234
Contact: Human Resources Program Coordinator

The region encompasses the historic trail gateway that was used by pioneers to cross the Cascade Mountains to the fertile coastal valley beyond. There are four major lakes, the Oregon Cascade Recreation Area, Mt. Thielsen Wilderness, and the Diamond Peak Wilderness in the forest. Located about 50 miles from Bend, Oregon, visitors come to enjoy the snow in winter and hiking, swimming and boating in the summer.

Volunteers are welcome at several different sites to help with campgrounds, visitor centers, interpretive walks, and trail maintenance.

Cost:
FREE.
Number of programs:
Several.
Age range:
Over 18.
Children:
No.
Major emphasis:
Service projects.
Sample programs:
Wilderness Rangers to collect data, July to September. *Trail Crews* for maintenance in summer, July to November. *Campground Hosts*, Memorial Day to Labor Day.
Provides:
Campsite, training, and full hook-ups provided.

ALSO:
Bureau of Land Management in Prineville/Deschutes/Central Oregon welcomes campground hosts and recreation staff assistants.
Contact:
BLM, PO Box 550, Prineville OR 97754
Phone: 503-447-4115

Oregon - Passport in Time

Address: Clearinghouse, PO Box 18364, Washington, DC 20036
Phone: 202-293-0922
Fax: 202-293-1782
Contact: Kathleen Schamel

Cost:
  FREE.
Number of programs:
  16.
Age range:
  18 and over.
Children:
  Over 16 on some programs.
Major emphasis:
  Historical research.
Sample programs:
  Scuba Diver for lake research. *Archaeological Assistants*. *Rebuild* historic site.
Provides:
  Varies. Campsites, camping, RVs.

Passport in Time invites volunteers to enjoy free vacations helping on a variety of historic preservation projects in Oregon.

Certified scuba divers are needed at the Paulina Lake Underwater Site. They will survey, map and sample a lake inside a volcanic caldera in the Newberry National Volcanic Monument with evidence of prehistoric occupation dating to 10,000 years ago.

In Deschutes National Forest, volunteers look for rock art, including pictographs and petroglyphs along Tumalo Creek. Also, at the Ogden Group Site Excavation they can dig small test excavations to determine the boundaries and depth of a prehistoric campsite.

In Fremont National Forest, volunteers will restore the Bald Butte Lookout built in 1931, and reconstruct the Bly Ranger Station compound which is on the National Register of Historic Places.

In the heart of Oregon's mining country, hundreds of Chinese miners lived in Wallowa-Whitman National Forest in the 1860s, searching for gold. Volunteers will survey and record artifact fragments of opium paraphernalia, woks, cooking oil cans, stoneware vessels, and ceramics, left behind in the meal preparation area. At the abandoned Chinese Two Dragon mining camp, volunteers will excavate three different structures.

Volunteers are needed on several archaeological and historical projects in Malheur National Forest, Siskiyou National Forest, Siuslaw National Forest, Umatilla National Forest, Umpqua National Forest, and Willamette National Forest.

Pacific Catalyst

Address: 444 Pine Street, Boulder, CO 80302
Phone: 303-442-0808
Contact: Holly Wheeler

When the *Catalyst* was discovered in Alaska, a group of friends bought it with the intent of offering ecology-oriented luxury cruises. Though not a truly bargain trip, you'll enjoy a unique inland water adventure aboard a restored 1932 research vessel, with room for 10 passengers and four crew members. There's a full-size galley, dining and meeting area, three bathrooms, five staterooms, and portholes in every cabin.

In the fall you explore the hundreds of San Juan Islands off the coast of Washington, with a wealth of birds and marine life including bald eagles, herons, Dall's porpoise, salmon, otters, seals, and Orca whales. In summer you tour Southeast Alaska to watch for whales and eagles, hike in moss-covered rain forests, and swim in natural hot springs. In winter, the boat is available for charter in Baja California.

Cost:
From $1,550 to $2,200.
Number of programs:
3.
Age range:
18 and up.
Children:
All ages welcome and special family trips available.
Major emphasis:
Naturalist cruises with learning.
Sample programs:
San Juan Islands, Washington, 7 days, $1,550. *Southeast Alaska*, 7 days, $2,200.
Provides:
Accommodations, all meals, excursions, guides, equipment, instruction, pre-trip material, tips.

Paragon Guides

Address: PO Box 130, Vail, CO 81658
Phone: 303-926-5299
Fax: 303-926-5298
Contact: Buck Elliott or Karen Peck

With 15 years of experience in backcountry adventures on Colorado's 10th Mountain Trail & Hut System, this company offers a variety of winter skiing vacations in Colorado. They also offer summer llama treks, mountain biking, and rock climbing adventures.

The 10th Mountain Trail is a backcountry trail and hut system developed between Aspen and Vail, in more than 400 square miles of Colorado. Modeled after the European Haute Route, the system was inspired by Fritz Benedict, whose vision and persistence opened the first huts in 1982. The huts are custom-built out of log or adapted from the materials in the area, and are located in pristine settings on leased National Forest land. They are equipped with woodburning cooking and heating stoves, solar light panels and outhouses with some exceptional views.

Trips range in length from 3-day weekends staying at one hut to 8-day trips skiing to several huts. Because the trails and huts are at high altitudes, and you ski with a pack weighing about 25 lbs., with altitude changes of 700 feet to 2,800 feet each day, basic intermediate skiing skills are required for all trips, and more advanced skiing skills for specific trips. Participants should be in good physical condition, take time to acclimate, and have a spirit for adventure.

Cost:
    $510 to $1,440.
Number of programs:
    5 programs, more than 50 trips.
Age range:
    3 to 80.
Children:
    Best ages: 5 and over.
Major emphasis:
    Quality backcountry adventures.
Sample programs:
    Backcountry Skiing, 3 days, $510.
    Mountain Biking Hut to Hut, 5 days, $1,000.
Provides:
    Accommodations, guides, equipment, instruction, pre-trip material, all meals, transportation on land.

"I've taken several trips, and I like everything about the experience—of course the fantastic scenery and skiing are hard to beat. They do a great job, are competent, knowledgeable, and fun!"
Ski trip participant from Nebraska

Passport in Time

Address: Clearinghouse, PO Box 18364, Washington DC 20036
Phone: 202-293-0922
Fax: 202-293-1782
Contact: Kathleen Schamel

Cost:
FREE. Non-profit organization.
Number of programs:
More than 100.
Age range:
18 and over.
Children:
Welcome on some projects with adult.
Major emphasis:
Historic preservation.
Sample programs:
See Passport in Time listings under *Arizona, California, Idaho, Michigan, Montana, New Mexico, Oregon, Utah*. Programs also offered in *Colorado, Georgia, Illinois, Minnesota, Missouri, Nebraska, North Carolina, North Dakota, South Carolina, South Dakota, Virginia, West Virginia, Wisconsin, Washington,* and *Wyoming*.
Provides:
Campsites, camping, lodging, RV sites, depending on program.

Free vacations working on historical and restoration projects with archaeologists and historians in national parks and historic sites in 23 states are available through Passport in Time.

You can document rock art in Coconino National Forest, Arizona. You can record the oral history of Oregon's range use in the 19th century by interviewing local ranchers. You can float Idaho's Salmon River in a raft looking for signs of early Native American inhabitants. You can rebuild a 1939 fire lookout constructed by the Civilian Conservation Corps in 1939 in California, to be used as an interpretive shelter on a trail.

Some projects require special skills, such as excavation, mapping, drawing and photography experience, while others require good physical condition because the site is at a high altitude or in a wilderness area. Complete descriptions are listed in *PIT Traveler*, a free newsletter sent on request.

PIT is a partnership between the USDA Forest Service, an agency of the Department of Agriculture, and a Washington company, CEHP Inc, which stands for Conservation, Environment, and Historic Preservation. PIT coordinates the volunteers, and all projects are under the supervision of a Forest Service Heritage staff person, and are operated, in many cases, in conjunction with universities. Volunteers usually receive free camping, or a site at Forest Service campgrounds, or can stay at nearby motels or bed and breakfasts.

"We successfully relocated seven homesteads that matched descriptions from archival records; five others were not found. The majority of remains were stone foundations, depressions, scattered logs, and house lumber."
Participant on project in Arizona

Pennsylvania State Parks

Address: Bureau of State Parks, PO Box 8551,
Harrisburg PA 17105-8551
Phone: 800-63-PARKS
Contact: Volunteer Director

The state's Volunteer In Parks program offers you an opportunity to help in the dozens of state parks throughout Pennsylvania. You can help visitors and answer questions, assist the park service with research activities, serve as a Campground Host, or serve in an office or other special capacity. Some volunteers help for a couple of hours a week while others spend a few days a week, or the entire summer.

Volunteers can assist with environmental education programs, historical programs, and visitor centers. Others can lead nature walks or offer interpretive programs. You can join trail crews for trail maintenance, assist at beach and swimming parks, or help with group programs.

Cost:
    FREE.
Number of programs:
    Many.
Age range:
    Over 18.
Children:
    No.
Major emphasis:
    Service projects.
Sample programs:
    Campground Hosts. Visitor Center Assistants. Trail Maintenance.
Provides:
    Campsite for campground hosts.

Pocono Environmental Education Center

Address: RR2, Box 1010, Dingmans Ferry, PA 18328
Phone: 718-828-2319
Fax: 717-828-9695
Contact: Tom Shimalla

Open year-round, PEEC offers family vacation camps with programs in nature study, hiking, and arts and crafts. There are also weekend seminars in backpacking, canoeing, birdwatching, geology, reptile and amphibian study, and a night hike to watch bats. A Native American Workshop includes storytellers, drummers, and dancers.

Set on a 38-acre campus in the Pocono Mountains of northeastern Pennsylvania, with residential facilities and access to over 200,000 acres of public lands, PEEC's mission is to provide education to increase awareness of the environment at an affordable price. It is the largest residential center in the Western hemisphere for environmental education.

Because of its location, there are many opportunities for outdoor environmental studies on the Delaware River and its banks, lowland and upland forests, scenic gorges, fields, a quarry with fossils, ravines, reservoirs, lakes, streams, ponds and acid bogs.

Volunteer Work Weekends in July and August offer free lodging in cabins, meals, and nature programs, in exchange for 10 hours of work at PEEC.

Cost:
$84 to $274. Non-profit organization.
Number of programs:
92.
Age range:
Infants to elderly.
Children:
Best ages: 5 to 17.
Major emphasis:
Environment.
Sample programs:
Pocono Paddling for Beginners, 3 days, $119. *Family Vacation Camp*, 5 days, $154. *Bird Watching Autumn Migration*, 6 days, $274.
Provides:
Accommodations, excursions, guides, equipment, instruction, all meals, transportation, indoor swimming pool.

Potomac Appalachian Trail Club

Address: PATC, 118 Park Street S.E., Vienna VA 22180
Phone: 703-242-0693
Contact: Heidi Forrest

This club is responsible for maintaining nearly 900 miles of trails including 272 miles of the Appalachian Trail in Virginia, Maryland, Pennsylvania, and the District of Columbia.

Every summer, you can join a one-week trail crew from May to September to work in Shenandoah National Park and George Washington National Forest.

Cost:
FREE.
Number of programs:
Every week in the summer.
Age range:
18 and over.
Children:
No.
Major emphasis:
Maintaining trails.
Sample programs:
Trail maintenance. Cabin restoration.
Provides:
Tent or cabin accommodations, all meals, small weekly stipend.

Roads Less Traveled

Address: **Biking & Hiking Adventures,**
PO Box 8187, Longmont, CO 80501
Phone: **303-678-8750**
Contact: **David Clair**

Cost:
From $675 to $1,245.
Number of programs:
About 30.
Age range:
All ages.
Children:
Best age: over 12.
Major emphasis:
Outdoor hiking, biking, rafting and horseback adventures.
Sample programs:
San Rafael Swell Explorer, bike and hike, 6 days, $675. *Colorado Hut to Hut*, biking, 6 days, $875. *Arizona Rambler*, hiking and rafting, 6 days, $1025.
Provides:
Accommodations, all meals and snacks, guides, vehicle support, waterbottle, daypack on trip, entrance fees, information packet.

David Clair and his staff lead bike and hike tours to forgotten backroads and dirt paths in the west. Here, there's still an unspoiled wilderness of emerald lakes, isolated ghost towns of the early pioneers, remote guest ranches, and herd of elk and deer. You might relax in natural hot springs, visit Indian pueblos, white-water raft and ride a horse.

Groups are limited to 13 people. Hiking is geared to an average adult who can walk between 6-10 miles a day on rolling terrain and gradual climbs. Bike tours are classified beginner, athletic beginner, and intermediate. Along the way, you usually stay in comfortable inns, though some trips offer camping and mountain hut stays.

In Colorado, a unique system of 12 huts built by the US Army's 10th Mountain Division circles the Holy Cross Wilderness and more than 300 miles of trails link the huts. Originally intended for cross-country skiers, the huts are now open in the summer to hikers and bikers and Clair's tour takes you through spectacular mountain scenery.

In Utah, the San Rafael Swell is a tremendous upheaval of rock with bizarre and unreal landscapes that you can explore on foot and on bike. Or tour Utah's Canyonlands to discover Indian petroglyphs and rock spires.

Other trips visit Arizona's Sonoran Desert, Bryce and Zion Canyons, and Yellowstone National Park. A challenging bike trip follows the Kokopelli Trail, which links Grand Junction, Colorado, and Moab, Utah, along a route that winds down 4,000-foot canyons and along narrow ridge tracks.

"Although we have been on bike trips before, never have we gotten off the road into the back country to see sights not available to the casual tourist." Participant on New Mexico trip

Rocky Mountain Nature Association

Address: Rocky Mountain National Park, Estes Park, CO 80517
Phone: 970-586-1258
Fax: 970-586-1310
Contact: Seminar Coordinator

Cost:
From $25 to $170. Non-profit organization.
Number of programs:
80 one-day to one-week seminars every year.
Age range:
18 to 80.
Children:
8 years and older at some seminars.
Major emphasis:
Natural and cultural history of Rocky Mountain National Park region.
Sample programs:
Llama Alternative, half day, $25; children 8 to 12 free. *Wildflower Identification*, one day, $50. *Winter Photography*, 2 ½ days, $100. *American Indian Women: Expressions of Beauty*, one week, $170.
Price includes:
Registration, instruction, pre-trip materials, guides, campsite.

Rocky Mountain Nature Association offers a variety of seminars in the park to help visitors understand what they are seeing. Every class is taught by an expert who has spent many years exploring the region. Most seminars require hiking. The high altitude and the variable weather can make hikes a challenge, and participants should be in good health.

Rocky Mountain National Park covers more than 400 square miles of mountain peaks, meadows, alpine tundra, trout-filled streams, and glacier-carved valleys. At 14,255 feet, Longs Peak juts up from a line of jagged mountain peaks against the sky.

There are day-long, multi-day, and week-long seminars on a variety of topics. Look for mammals of the Rockies with Dr. Bruce Wunder, chair of the department of biology at Colorado State University. Study Rocky Mountain history and visit historical sites with C. W. Buchholtz, author of a history of the park. Enjoy hikes to examine grasses, sedges, mosses, lichens, and ferns with Dr. Beatrice Willard, who created the seminar program in 1962. Campsites are available in the park or you can stay in hotels nearby.

Other seminars cover nature photography, butterflies, watercolor painting, and American Indian women. Day trips focus on mountain insects, edible and useful plants, mushrooms, wildflower identification, and flintknapping.

Saga Holidays

Address: 222 Berkeley Street, Boston, MA 02116
Phone: 800-343-0273
Contact: Office

Cost:
$999 to $2,549.
Number of programs:
15 in US and Canada.
Age range:
50 and over.
Children:
Under 50 permitted if accompanied by parent or guardian who is over 50.
Major emphasis:
Affordable vacations for mature travelers.
Sample programs:
Music of the Heartland, Missouri & Ozarks, 7 nights, $999. *National Parks of the West*, 14 nights, $1,749. *British Columbia and the Inside Passage*, 14 nights, $2,099.
Provides:
Airfare, accommodations, most meals, tour director, medical and other insurance, transportation, excursions, entry fees, local guides, taxes, pre-trip information.

"Our travelers are over the age of 50, enjoying the prime of life," notes a staff member. "They want to visit new destinations, meet new people, and return home enriched by the experience."

Saga Holidays began in England 42 years ago and the company has been offering holidays worldwide for mature American travelers since 1980. It rarely advertises and does not work with travel agents. Instead, brochures are sent directly to travelers, who book their vacations. Saga has twice received the Queen's Award for Export Achievement in England, and in the USA was named to Boston Better Business Bureau's President's Honor Roll, for having "upheld the highest sense of business ethics and customer satisfaction."

There's a choice of coach tours, stay-in-one-place vacations, cruises, and educational travel programs. Once a year, there's a week-long Saga Jamboree, a reunion for travelers.

There are several tours in the US and Canada. Visit the Shenandoah Valley and Cape Hatteras; explore Yosemite National Park and the California coastline; see the Northwest with trips to Glacier and Mt. Rainier national parks and a snow coach ride on a glacier; or travel through Missouri, Arkansas, and Tennessee and stop at St. Louis, Graceland, and a blues show in Memphis. There's also a cruise through British Columbia's Inside Passage, a trans-continental train ride, and a tour of Victoria and Vancouver.

"I traveled alone with Saga and that's the big test. I always felt they did a great job." Participant from Florida

Sierra Club Service Trips

Address: 730 Polk Street, San Francisco, CA 94109
Phone: 415-776-2211
Contact: Service Outings Director

The Sierra Club, founded in 1892, has been a leader in outdoor adventure vacations for many years. A detailed list of national and international Outings is published every January in their magazine.

Least expensive are Service Trips, which are subsidized by the National Outings Committee. Energetic and enthusiastic people can do something positive for the environment while enjoying the outdoors. Often organized in conjunction with the Forest Service and National Park Service, volunteers build and maintain trails, repair meadows, help archaeologists, and clean up debris. On most trips, half the days are left free to enjoy the wilderness. There's usually a a trip cook, and meals are renowned for their excellence.

While programs vary from year to year, here's a sampling of what you can do:

√ Stay at a base camp in North Carolina and improve trails, build a walking bridge, and enjoy the brilliant colors of spring wildflowers in full bloom.

√ From a campsite 9,000 feet up on Cloud Peak in the Bighorn National Forest of Wyoming, you construct trails and enjoy great fishing, wildlife, and dramatic views.

√ On Maryland's Eastern Shore, clear land on the Nature Conservancy's creek preserve, and join an archaeological dig at a historic town site.

√ In the Arkansas Ozarks, build a segment of a new hiking trail along the Buffalo River, America's first national river.

Some Service Trips have doctors on staff, who donate their time and skillls for a fee waiver, and medical professionals are welcome to apply. All trip leaders have first aid training.

Cost:
$190 to $385.
Number of programs:
Many.
Age range:
All ages.
Children:
Depends on project.
Major emphasis:
Preserving the environment.
Sample programs:
Acadia Park, Maine, 7 days, $195. *Big Sur, Ventana Wilderness*, California, 9 days, $245. *Paria Canyon Archaeology*, Arizona, 8 days, $325.
Provides:
Accommodations, transportation, all meals, guides, instruction, equipment.

Smithsonian Study Tours

Address: Smithsonian Institution,
1100 Jefferson Drive SW, Washington, DC 20560
Phone: 202-357-4700
Fax: 202-786-2315
Contact: Prudence Clendenning

Cost:
From $725 to $3,980.
Number of programs:
More than 100.
Age range:
18 and over.
Children:
Welcome on some programs.
Major emphasis:
Educational travel.
Sample programs:
Big Bend National Park, Texas, 9 days, $1,175. *Hawaii's Trails and Reefs*, 12 days, $1,995. *Waterways of the Pacific Northwest*, 7 days, $2,580.
Provides:
Accommodations, some meals, excursions, guides, lecturers, pre-trip material, transportation.

Dozens of affordable tours led by expert naturalists, historians and environmentalists are offered by the Smithsonian. More than 350 tours and seminars around the world led by experts in the field are available throughout the year.

In the United States, you can experience the natural sculpture of Bryce Canyon National Park, the cliffs of Zion National Park and the Grand Canyon in Arizona; study Native American Art in the southwest; go hiking in Great Smoky Mountains National Park between North Carolina and Tennessee; or join a guided hiking tour through Yellowstone National Park in Wyoming. Cruises tour Alaska's Coastal Wilderness, the waterways of the Pacific Northwest from Vancouver to Seattle, or travel along the Columbia and Snake Rivers, following the epic exploration route of Lewis and Clark.

You can also visit Texas, Idaho, Florida, the California desert, and Hawaii, among other programs. There's a tour of Maryland's homes and gardens, and a spring tour of the Gardens of the Delaware Valley.

Research Expeditions invite travelers to work with scientists on projects such as assisting astronomers at Mt. Wilson Observatory in California, helping with the National Numismatics Collection in Washington, DC, and documenting the Annual Crow Fair in Billings, Montana.

"When I thought of all we received for the money, it was not only great, but very economical."
Participant on New Orleans program

Student Conservation Association

Address: PO Box 550, Charlestown, NH 03603
Phone: 603-543-1700
Fax: 603-543-1828
Contact: Joyce Rodgers, Recruiting Manager.

Cost:
FREE. Non-profit organization.
Number of programs:
8.
Age range:
16 and over.
Children:
No.
Major emphasis:
Hands-on environmental work.
Sample programs:
Resource Assistant Program, adults, all expenses paid. *High School Program,* 16-18 years, pay travel from home to site.
Provides:
Accommodations in tent, all meals, equipment, training. Financial aid available for those in need. Backpacks and sleeping bags can be borrowed.

The SCA, founded in 1957, provides high school and college students and other adults with the chance to volunteer their services in national parks, public lands, and natural and cultural resources. SCA programs are held in cooperation with the National Park Service, US Forest Service, Bureau of Land Management, US Fish & Wildlife Service, state parks, and private organizations. There are two options:

Resource Assistants who work in a professional capacity for 12 weeks. RA positions offer a variety of tasks, generally in a specific area such as archaeology, history, wilderness management, forestry, geology, or trail maintenance, among others. If you're considering a career in natural resources, this is an excellent way to gain hands-on experience outdoors.

High School Program for students from across the country, for 4 to 5 weeks. The students join environmental work groups with up to 10 participants and one or two adult supervisors, and complete outdoor work projects such as site restoration, trail construction, and repairing fences. They live in backcountry locations as part of a cooperating group, and take part in a major week-long expedition. Leaders encourage identification of flowers and plants, study of geology, discussion of environmental issues, and use of low-impact camping techniques.

In 1993, 476 students participated in the High School Program at 68 locations, including building a hiking trail with wheelchair access in Michigan. Also, 1,151 Resource Assistants filled a wide range of services including reconstruction in Florida's Everglades National Park to repair hurricane damage.

Sundance Expeditions & Kayak School

Address: 14894 Galice Road, Merlin, OR 97532
Phone: 503-479-8508
Fax: 503-476-6565
Contact: Judo Patterson

Whitewater kayak instruction and multiday raft adventures are the specialty of this company, in operation since 1973. Kayak programs are designed for all levels of expertise.

The nine-day beginner program starts with five days of paddling and practicing various strokes including the Eskimo roll on sections of the Rogue River. During these training days, students enjoy the hot tub, sauna, and massage, meals and lodging at the Sundance River House. The last four days they take a kayak river trip down the rapids and riffles with camping along the way.

Non-paddling spouses or friends don't have to get in the water. They can relax at the River House, or hike the trails that start just outside the door.

Intermediate kayakers can sign up for the last five days of the beginners' program, or choose specially designed instructional programs.

Advanced kayakers have two warm-up days on the Rogue followed by a three-day raft-supported trip on Oregon's Class IV Wild & Scenic Illinois River.

"If you want to learn to kayak, it is our job and our pleasure to provide the avenue for you to do so, and to keep you safe and comfortable while you learn a new sport," says Judo Patterson. "Kayaking is a skill-intensive sport: You need to be pretty good at it to be able to start enjoying it."

Cost:
From $795 to $1,350.
Number of programs:
48.
Age range:
14 to 60
(kayakers' average age, 35-50).
Children:
14 and over for kayak school.
Sample programs:
Rogue River Raft Trip, 4 days, $450.
Intermediate Kayak Program, 4 days, $795. *Beginner Kayak Program*, 9 days, $1,350.
Provides:
Accommodations, all meals, excursions, guides, equipment, instruction, pre-trip material, transportation on land.

"The diverse scenery, deep pools and rolling rapids I had experienced around every bend of the Rogue River had become a part of me I would not soon forget." Participant from New York

Texas - Aransas National Wildlife Refuge

Address: PO Box 100, Austwell, TX 77950
Phone: 512-286-3559 or 286-3533
Fax: 512-286-3722
Contact: Volunteer Coordinator

Established in 1937 to protect the vanishing wildlife of coastal Texas, this is an ever-changing region still being shaped by the tides and storms of the Gulf of Mexico. The 54,829-acre refuge spreads over the Blackjack Peninsula, named after the scattered blackjack oaks. There are grasslands, live oaks, and tidal marshes as well as ponds, home to cranes, alligators, and other wildlife.

Thousand of migratory birds fly to the refuge on their journey between North and Central America, and in mild winters you can see pelicans, egrets, spoonbills, ducks and geese. The endangered whooping crane also comes to the saltwater marshes. The numbers of cranes is now over 100, from a low of 15 birds in 1941. The birds arrive in late October and stay until mid-April, and are sometimes spotted from the Observation Tower or the fishing pier at Goose Island State Park.

The refuge needs volunteers to help with a wide variety of jobs. These include visitor information, preparing interpretive materials, work with youth groups, trail maintenance, carpentry, computer services, bird identification, library slide file organization, and environmental education. Positions are available year-round. A commitment of 32 hours a week on a four-day schedule is required.

Cost:
    FREE.
Number of programs:
    Many.
Age range:
    Over 18.
Children:
    No.
Major emphasis:
    Service projects.
Sample programs:
    Visitor Center staff.
    Trail Maintenance.
    Office Work with computers.
Provides:
    Trailer/RV site with complete hookups. Laundry facilities. Use of government vehicle on refuge.

ALSO:
    Texas State Parks welcome volunteers as Park Hosts for a month or longer to help with operations and maintenance. Free trailer site.
Contact:
    Public Lands Division,
    Texas Parks & Wildlife Dept.,
    4200 Smith School Road,
    Austin TX 78744
    Phone: 512-389-4415

Timberline Bicycle Tours

Address: 7975 E. Harvard, Unit J, Denver, CO 80231
Phone: 303-759-3804
Fax: 303-368-1651
Contact: Dick Gottsegen

For the past 12 years, Carol and Dick Gottsegen have led Timberline bike trips in the West, and just recently they introduced some hiking trips too.

"We truly believe that you've never really experienced an area until you've experienced the joy and pride of doing so as the product of your own power and spirit," they say. "The cyclist and hiker alike see not only the breathtaking beauty of a region; each also feels the land, senses the crispness of the air, the sound of rushing waters, the scent of alpine flora."

Dozens of trips ride through Montana's Glacier Park, Yellowstone National Park, northern New Mexico's Santa Fe-Taos region, the magnificent Canadian Rockies, Nova Scotia, Utah's canyons, Idaho's wilderness, the Oregon coastline, Colorado's high country, California, South Dakota, and more.

Bikers stay in comfortable lodgings, often in historic inns or mountain lodges with swimming pools, tubs, or whatever you need to soothe your tired muscles. Breakfast and dinners are always provided, and lunch on mountain bike and hike tours. On other bike trips, travelers can stop where they want for lunch, or choose to picnic on the way.

Six hikes visit the Grand Canyon, Montana, Washington, and Canada. Hiking tours are inn-to-inn, and you often stay in the magnificent lodges distinct to each hiking area, such as the Phantom Ranch in the Grand Canyon.

Cost:
  $795 to $1,395.
Number of programs:
  130.
Age range:
  12 to 72.
Children:
  13 and older.
Major emphasis:
  Cycling, on and off-road, and hiking.
Sample programs:
  Grand Canyon, Arizona, hiking, 6 days, $925. *Yellowstone Alpiner, Wyoming,* biking, 7 days, $1050. *Glacier Park Rambler, Montana,* biking, 9 days, $1,195. *Canadian Rockies,* biking, 10 Days, $1,395.
Provides:
  Accommodations, most meals, guides, pre-trip material, tips, transportation on land, support van.

"Enjoyed everything about the trip. This was an especially beautiful ride, not too hard, long days so lots of exercise, good group, good weather. Hope to do it again."
Participant on biking trip, Utah

University Research Expeditions Program

Address: University of California, Berkeley, CA 94720-7050
Phone: 510-642-6586
Fax: 510-642-6791
Contact: Jean Colvin

Cost:
$790 to $1,295.
Number of programs:
Most abroad, a few in USA.
Age range:
All ages.
Children:
No.
Major emphasis:
Assist research projects in the field.
Sample programs:
Water and the Future of California, 14 days, $790. *Native American Health Care*, Trinidad, 14 days, $1,160. *Dinosaurs in Montana*, 14 days, $1,295.
Provides:
Accommodations, all meals, transportation, camping, field gear, research equipment, reading lists, instruction. Contributions to expeditions are tax-deductible.

Here's a way to enjoy a research adventure that can't be found anywhere else. You don't need any special academic or field experience to participate. Curiosity, adaptability, and willingness to share the costs and lend a helping hand are the most important qualifications.

UREP, established in 1976, specializes in matching interested people from all walks of life with University of California scholars in need of assistance on research expeditions worldwide. UREP has sponsored hundreds of field teams in more than 50 countries. More than 400 volunteers are involved every year on research projects.

While the majority of projects are abroad in Europe, Ecuador, India, East Africa, Belize, Panama, and Easter Island among others, there are some programs in the United States. In the California, Isleton and Sacramento River Delta, you help measure the effects of water diversion on the local ecosystem, rural economy, and way of life, in an effort to develop a truer vision of the cost and effect of water policy in the West.

In Trinidad, Northern California, there is a model program run by the United Indian Health Services for the prevention and treatment of diabetes in the Native American population; volunteers assist by interviewing clinic staff and gathering population data to examine this widespread problem in an environmental, cultural, and political context. And in Montana, you assist paleontologists on a dinosaur dig, excavating fossils.

"It was a wonderful introduction to archaeological field work. I'm hooked for life." Business woman participant

Utah - Canyonlands National Park

Address: 2282 Southwest Resource Boulevard, Moab, UT 84532
Phone: 801-259-3911
Contact: Betty S. White

A wilderness of more than 330,000 acres in southeastern Utah, this is a country of dramatic landscapes, lush canyons and vivid colors. The geologic diversity and the stunning beauty of the scenery is breathtaking. Three districts—Island in the Sky, Needles, and Maze—are created by the confluence of the Green and Colorado rivers, which are popular for rafting. The areas have hiking, biking, and off-road-vehicle trails.

Volunteer positions include resource management assistants, who help with revegetation and water projects, and hiking trails repair and maintenance staff. Training and tools are provided. If you love the outdoors and meeting people, you can volunteer to answer visitors' questions and organize interpretive programs.

Cost:
FREE.
Number of programs:
Several.
Age range:
Over 18.
Children:
No.
Major emphasis:
Service projects.
Sample programs:
Visitor Center Assistant, Island in the Sky. *Backcountry Trail Counters*, Needles.
Revegetation, Arches and Needles areas.
Provides:
Trailer/RV pad with complete hookups for working 30 hours a week or more.

ALSO:
Bureau of Land Management is responsible for wilderness areas in several regions of Utah. Volunteers are welcome as recreation assistants, backcountry patrols, and campground hosts. In Moab District's Price River Resource Area, a Paleontology Aide assists with a dinosaur dig at the Cleveland Lloyd Quarry.
Contact:
BLM/Price River Resource Area, 900 North 700 East, Price UT 84501
Phone: 801-637-4584

"There's a lot of work that needs to be done out in the parks that wouldn't ordinarily get done. As a volunteer, I can help by doing some of the work."
Participant in Canyonlands National Park, Utah

Utah - Passport in Time

Address: Clearinghouse, PO Box 18364, Washington, DC 20036
Phone: 202-293-0922
Fax: 202-293-1782
Contact: Kathleen Schamel

Passport in Time invites volunteers to enjoy free vacations helping on a variety of historic preservation projects in Utah.

An ongoing survey of the High Uintas Mountains in Ashley National Forest continues as volunteers look for and record interesting prehistoric and historic sites at elevations of 10,000 feet in the Chepeta Lake area. They will also restore the Oscar Swett homestead to turn it into an interpretive center.

Abandoned gold mines in Bullion Canyon mark the sites of many former settlements, including those of the Spanish Conquistadors. Volunteers will construct a log cabin on the Miners Park Historical Trail, and also attempt to recover a wooden ore car from the slopes below the mine. In the evenings, there are campfire chats with retired miners.

A mining boom in American Fork Canyon in 1871 created the town of Forest City, which closed down in 1878 when the boom ended. Volunteers will search for structural foundations and artifacts, and produce a town map.

In Fishlake National Forest, volunteers working with an archaeologist will test a 1,000-year-old wickiup site that suggests the presence of hunters at Fish Lake about 10,000 years ago.

Cost:
    FREE.
Number of programs:
    6.
Age range:
    18 and over.
Children:
    Over 16 on some programs.
Major emphasis:
    Historic preservation.
Sample programs:
    Construction Work on old buildings. *Mapping* mining town. *Archaeology Assistants.*
Provides:
    Campsites, camping, RV sites.

Vermont State Parks

Address: 103 South Main Street, Waterbury, VT 05671-0603
Phone: 802-241-3655
Fax: 802-244-1481
Contact: Larry T. Simino

You can have a free volunteer stay in any of the 45 parks comprising the Vermont State Park System and ranging from rolling mountains to developed beach areas, with boat rentals and concessions, as well as hiking trails. The parks have 2,200 campsites available.

The Host/Volunteer Program welcomes volunteers to help with the operations and maintenance of the parks during the season. You will be provided with a free RV site in exchange for a minimum of 20 hours of work a week, or 30 hours for couples.

What can you do? At visitor centers, volunteers provide information on local activities and sights, explain safety precautions and regulations in the parks, share information about other state parks, and may help with registration.

You can develop programs or assist as performers in special programs to educate and entertain visitors in historical or cultural events.

Active volunteers maintain, clean, repair and upgrade trails, campsites, rest rooms, lawns, flower beds, and park facilities and equipment. Some volunteers assist in research projects into the region's natural, archaeological, historical and cultural resources.

Cost:
FREE. Non-profit organization.
Number of programs:
One.
Age range:
16 to 70.
Children:
16 and over.
Major emphasis:
Volunteer work in state parks.
Sample programs:
6 weeks commitment desired, free campsite. Work required: 20 hours for individuals, 30 hours for couples.
Provides:
Campsite, RV site.

"Volunteers in Vermont State Parks are a welcome addition to our State Park System. We owe a great debt of gratitude to those who become VVSPs."
A staff member

Victor Emanuel Nature Tours

Address: PO Box 33008, Austin TX 78764
Phone: 800-328-VENT: 512-328-5221
Fax: 512-328-2919
Contact: Ted Siff

VENT, founded in 1976, specializes in small group tours led by expert birders and naturalists, many of whom are the foremost experts in their field. You choose a tour from the dozens in the catalog, which is illustrated with wonderful drawings and photographs of birds, animals, and scenery.

About 60 percent of VENT participants are repeat travelers, and some people have been on a dozen trips. New birders are always welcome, and tours in Texas, Arizona, and Florida are recommended for beginners. VENT is also involved in local conservation efforts, such as protecting the El Triunfo Cloud Forest reserve in Mexico.

In the United States, you can look for and listen to the nightbirds of Arizona, including Strickland's woodpecker and the red-faced warbler. In Colorado, you can spot the four species of grouse that inhabit the prairies of North America. In Texas, the migration of birds over High Island on the coast offers the chance to see as many as 25 species of warblers. In Yellowstone National Park, a fall trip looks for marsh and waterfowl including trumpeter awans as well as moose, elk, mule deer, bighorn sheep and bison.

The North Puget Sound region of Washington and nearby British Columbia is the winter home for birds of prey, diving birds, waterfowl, and land birds. In Montana, which has the largest number of breeding owl species in North America, you join experts from the Owl Research Institute to help their study of long-eared owls. In Hawaii, you look for Hawaiian forest birds, as well as seabirds nesting in the remote Pacific.

Trips abroad visit Bolivia, Brazil, Belize, Argentina, Mexico, Australia, New Zealand, Papua New Guinea, India and China among others.

"When I went on this trip, I was a little skeptical. But I couldn't have been happier. Not only did we find the most amazing birds, but the group was the best bunch of birders I've ever spent time with." Teenager on Papua New Guinea/Fiji trip

Cost:
From $695 to $2,655.
Number of programs:
More than 140, about 50 in North America.
Age range:
15 to 90.
Children:
14 or older, accompanied by parent.
Major emphasis:
Quality birding and nature expeditions.
Sample trips:
Arizona Hummingbirds, 7 days, $875. *Spring in South Texas*, 12 days, $1,395. *California & Arizona*, 13 days, $1,725.
Price includes:
Accommodations, all meals, transportation, guide service.

Virginia - George Washington National Forest

Address: PO Box 233, Harrisonburg VA 22801
Phone: 703-564-8300
Contact: Vicki A. Glover

A million acres of forest, mountains, and valleys spread across Virginia and West Virginia just an hour from Washington DC. The region includes part of the Shenandoah Valley and the Allegheny and Blue Ridge Mountains, and has a strong historical background with many routes used by Native Americans, and early explorers, and as Civil War battlegrounds.

Volunteers are welcome at a variety of different sites. Campground hosts and recreation aides assist at two campsites in the Dry River area. Near Gathright Dam/Lake Moomaw, which is a 2,500-acre expanse of water in the mountains, you can serve as a Wilderness Ranger. In the Lee District, you can volunteer as an Information Aide at a visitor center, or as a campground host. There's also an 1830s cabin built as the headquarters for the Elizabeth Iron Furnace that needs serious rehabilitation.

Cost:
  FREE.
Number of programs:
  Several.
Age range:
  Over 18.
Children:
  No.
Major emphasis:
  Service projects.
Sample programs:
  Campground Hosts at lakefront sites. *Carpenters* to restore historic cabin. *Information Aide* for visitor center.
Provides:
  Free campsite with water and electric hookup. Carpentry positions provide tools, training, housing, and campsite.

Virginia Dept. of Conservation & Recreation

Address: 203 Governor Street, Suite 306, Richmond, VA 23219
Phone: 804-371-2675
Contact: L. Paige Tucker

Cost:
 FREE.
Number of programs:
 Several.
Age range:
 All ages.
Children:
 Depends on project.
Major emphasis:
 Preserving state parks.
Sample programs:
 Campground Hosts at lakefront sites. *Maintenance and Carpentry* assistants.
Provides:
 Free campsite with water and electric hookup.

For people who cannot spend a month or the whole season as a volunteer, Virginia offers a new *7-for-7* program. In exchange for volunteering 40 hours a week during a week's stay (80 hours per couple, 130 per family) participants can camp for free for seven nights, and, in some parks, can extend their stay for up to three weeks.

The Department manages 40 state parks and natural areas in all regions of the Commonwealth. Volunteers are welcome to assist in a variety of positions in 14 of them, both indoor and outdoor. Activities include landscaping, maintenance, visitor services, and monitoring natural areas, among others.

The parks vary from Clayton Lake State Park in the mountains with wooded trails and boating, to Kiptopeke State Park along the Atlantic coast with a huge migratory bird population and a coastal dunes environment, to Southwest Virginia Museum in Big Stone Gap, which chronicles the exploration and development of the area.

Campground Hosts greet and help campers, and do light maintenance, and camp free for 30 to 90 days at selected parks, but must provide their own camping equipment or RV.

All volunteers can use the park facilities free where available including boating and fishing. Based on the number of hours served, volunteers receive a one-year or lifetime pass to all Virginia State Parks, camping and cabin use privileges, and certificates.

Volunteers for Outdoor Colorado (VOC)

Address: 1410 Grant Street, Suite B105, Denver, CO 80203
Phone: 303-830-7792
Fax: 303-8332-6056
Contact: Volunteer Director

Absolutely free outdoor volunteer vacations in Colorado are available through Volunteers for Outdoor Colorado. In April, VOC publishes an annual booklet that describes the weekend volunteer projects and other opportunities available through the Clearinghouse. Call VOC for the booklet, decide where you'd like to help and ask for any additional information you need.

VOC offers projects in partnership with other agencies on various weekends between April and October. Projects vary every year and include urban tree plantings, park enhancements, trail building and maintenance, and high-altitude wilderness experience. You provide your own camping equipment, transportation and personal gear.

VOC also maintains a Clearinghouse of individual and group volunteer opportunities with land management agencies around the state. Programs can last one day, one week or the entire summer. If you stay for the season, you usually get housing and a small stipend from the sponsoring agency.

Some positions demand special skills. You can assist archaeologists at the BLM Anasazi Heritage Center for one to three months. You can be a Backcountry Wilderness Host or a Campground Host at sites throughout Colorado. You can work on a trail crew in the high country as an interpreter with the National Park Service.

Cost:
   FREE. Non-profit organization.
Number of programs:
   Many.
Age range:
   8 to 85.
Children:
   Depends on project.
Major emphasis:
   Volunteer improvement projects on public lands.
Sample programs:
   Garden of the Gods Trail Project, 2 days. *Revegetating* high altitude trails, Leadville District, one week. *Northern Goshawk Nesting Survey*, Glenwood Springs, 1 to 2 months.
Provides:
   Clearinghouse positions: varies with project. Some provide housing and stipend. VOC Weekend Projects: usually free camping, meals and entertainment.

"No experience is necessary - just a willingness and desire to work hard and give something back."   A staff member

Volunteers for Outdoor Washington (VOW)

Address: Iron Goat Trail,
4516 University Way NE, Seattle, WA 98105
Phone: 206-283-1440: 206-545-4868 (VOW).
Contact: Sam Frey/Janet Wall

The Iron Goat Trail is situated in the Stevens Pass Historic District in the North Cascades mountains. The trail follows the abandoned loop of the Great Northern Railroad, closed in 1929, whose logo was an Iron Goat.

The route over Stevens Pass opened up the Pacific Northwest to settlers and immigrants. The railroad was one of the marvels of 19th century engineering with its intricate set of switchbacks cut into the mountains, but it limited trains to 600 tons. To avoid the switchbacks, the Cascade Tunnel was built in 1900, and snowsheds were erected after snowslide disasters. As rail traffic increased, a new eight-mile-long tunnel was built in 1929, and is still in use today.

Along the steep old railbed are many historic remainders, and trail enthusiasts meet for occasional History Get-Togethers to share photos, slides, maps and documents. Exploratory field hikes are also held.

The trail is being built largely by volunteers, under the auspices of Volunteers for Outdoor Washington and with the partnership of the US Forest Service. Four miles of the main trail have been completed. The second phase is an extension of the trail to the abandoned town of Wellington.

Volunteers are welcome to join work parties on weekends and some weekdays from May to October. Carpooling is available from Seattle. Hardhats will be provided, and the work is challenging. Call for information.

Volunteers for Outdoor Washington offers training workshops, sponsors clean-up parties at parks, and maintains and constructs many other trails beside the Iron Goat. There are various opportunities for volunteers.

Cost:
FREE.
Number of programs:
Weekends/weekdays trail work, May to October.
Age range:
Over 18.
Children:
No.
Major emphasis:
Creating new trail.
Sample programs:
Clearing trail.
Constructing drainage.
Provides:
Hardhats if required.

Volunteers for Peace

Address: 43 Tiffany Road, Belmont, VT 05730
Phone: 802-259-2759
Fax: 802-259-2922
Contact: Peter Coldwell, Director

Cost:
About $150 for 2-3 week program. Non-profit organization.

Number of programs:
800 a year approximately, 43 in USA.

Age range:
18 and up.

Children:
16 and 17-year-olds in France and Germany.

Major emphasis:
Environment, archaeology, reconstruction, children, handicapped.

Sample programs:
Moosehorn National Wildlife Refuge, Maine, environmental, 3 weeks. *Harmony School, Indiana*, work with children, 2 weeks. *Genesis Farm, New Jersey*, renovation and ecology, 2 weeks.

Provides:
Accommodations, all meals, some excursions.

For more than 70 years, workcamps have been an inexpensive and personal way to travel, live, and work in an international setting. VFP's mission is "to promote international goodwill through friendship and community service."

Though the majority of programs are abroad, there are 43 workcamps in the United States. Often volunteers come from other countries to work at these sites. Prairie Peace Park in Lincoln, Nebraska, welcomes volunteers to lead visitors on tours of the exhibits, help maintain the park, and meet peace groups, Native Americans, and others in the area.

In Washington, DC, the Community for Creative Non-Violence plans a Summer of Social Action for eight weeks to renovate homeless shelters, work in food kitchens, and visit inner city agencies. In Cordova, Alaska, at an environmental workcamp, volunteers will construct a boardwalk across wetlands and maintain trails. In Los Altos Hills, California, help is needed at a multiracial children's farm camp for 9 to 17-year-olds, and with organic gardening and land cultivation.

Program descriptions are listed in the International Workcamp Directory, ($12) published in April, with more than 800 announcements of openings for volunteers. People are advised to register as soon as possible to get their first choice because the majority of volunteers sign up between mid-April and mid-May.

In 1994, VFP placed about 1,000 people in workcamps. About 20 percent of the people who register every year spend several months abroad at different workcamps. Volunteers may be housed in a campsite, school, church, private home, or community center, and share and coordinate food preparation, projects, and recreation.

"You can help change the course of our planet in a personal way through the challenges of hands-on work projects and group living, and create a more positive vision for the world and the future."
VFP staff member

Washington State Parks & Recreation

Address: **Volunteers, 7150 Cleanwater Lane, Olympia WA 98504**
Phone: **206-753-5759**
Contact: **Volunteer Director**

This beautiful region of magnificent mountains and spectacular coastline has a wide range of openings for volunteers in parks around the state. At campgrounds, you can serve as a host and assist campers, provide information, and do minor maintenance. You can also work at an interpretive center, present education programs and scenic river programs, and teach boating safety instruction. While many positions are outdoors in the parks, you can also serve as a volunteer in the regional offices and the main headquarters.

For people over 55, the Senior Environmental Corps has openings in a range of projects where you monitor water quality, observe wildlife, and assist researchers.

Cost:
    FREE.
Number of programs:
    Several.
Age range:
    Over 18. Some programs for 55 and over.
Children:
    No.
Major emphasis:
    Service projects.
Sample programs:
    Campground Hosts. Boating Instructors. Office Assistants.
Provides:
    Campsite with minimum of 28 hours a week of service. Hook-ups in most parks, but need own camping unit.

ALSO:
    Volunteers are needed in national forests in Washington through the USDA Forest Service, Pacific Northwest Regional Office, Region Six.
Contact:
    PO Box 3623,
    Portland, Oregon 97208
    Phone: 503-326-3816
    Contact: Drinda Lombardi

Windjammer Cruises Victory Chimes

Address: PO Box 1401, Rockland ME 04841
Phone: 207-594-0755
Fax: 207-265-5651
Contact: Captain Kip Files

The largest windjammer under the US flag, *Victory Chimes* sails from Rockland, Maine across spectacular Penobscot Bay, and graciously cruises among the pine-dotted islands and peninsulas. Overnight, she stops at out-of-the-way coves, popular resort towns, and fishing villages that have hardly changed since the 1900s when the vessel was built.

This stately three-masted 170-foot schooner once hauled cargo up and down Chesapeake Bay until she was abandoned in a Maryland shipyard. In 1954, she was brought to Maine and restored by Captain Guild, who sailed her in Maine's windjammer fleet until he retired. She was then bought by Domino's Pizza. A complete overhaul was ordered, supervised by a young Maine seaman, Kip Files, and his boss at Domino's, Paul DeGaeta. In 1990 they bought the boat to sail along the Maine coast every summer.

There's room for 40 passengers, who are welcome to help hoist and lower the sails, or practice navigational skills with compass and chart. The comfortable cabins all have a port hole and sink with hot and cold running water, and there's electricity, hot showers, push-button toilets and central hot-air furnace. Meals include fresh blueberry pancakes, lobsters, and delicious New England menus.

"She is one of a kind, a real national treasure, and sailing on her is taking part in an historical event that stays with you," says Captain Files.

Cost:
$350 to $650.
Number of programs:
20 sailings, June to September.
Age range:
All ages.
Children:
Welcome.
Major emphasis:
Sailing cruises along the Maine coast.
Sample programs:
Getaway Cruise, 3 days, $350. *Race Week Cruise*, 5 days, $600. *Summer Cruise*, 6 days, $650.
Provides:
Accommodations, all meals, guides, excursions.

"The scenery was breathtaking. I spent my time reading, relaxing and laughing with the other passengers. I highly recommend sailing on a windjammer for anyone's who feeling adventurous or needs some peaceful relaxation time."
Participant from Boston

Wisconsin - Apostle Islands National Lakeshore

Address: Route 1, Box 4, Bayfield, WI 54814
Phone: 715-779-3397
Contact: Bill Ferraro

Cost:
FREE.
Number of programs:
Several.
Age range:
Over 18.
Children:
No.
Major emphasis:
Preservation projects.
Sample programs:
Lighthouse Keeper, May to October. *Campground Hosts*, minimum stay 2 months. *Bird Observer,* flexible 40 hours a week.
Provides:
Accommodations possible, sometimes transportation, equipment.

ALSO:
Wisconsin Department of Natural Resources looks after 70 state parks, recreation areas and trails where volunteers are welcome. Campground Host positions are available at 45 state parks, as well as trail maintenance, interpretive work, and patrols.
Contact:
Department of Natural Resources, Box 7921, Madison WI 53707
Phone: 608-266-2152
Contact: Norman Pazderski

Apostle Islands National Lakeshore consists of 21 islands off the northern tip of Wisconsin in Lake Superior. Some of the islands have old fishing and logging camps, stone quarries and other reminders of the era when people lived and worked there. Today, you find hiking trails and wilderness camping.

The park has five lighthouses built around 1900 and once inhabited by working lighthouse keepers and their families. Every summer volunteers serve as lighthouse keepers and live there for "five months of peace and solitude." The housing is rustic but comfortable.

Volunteers mow the lawns, do light housekeeping, hike the trails, greet occasional visitors, give guided tours, and administer first aid if needed. There is no electricity or running water, so kerosene lamps and privies are provided. All drinking water has to be brought from the mainland, but there's plenty of water for other purposes in the lake. The water is extremely cold for would-be swimmers.

Other volunteer positions available for the summer are bird observers, museum computer operator, campground host, photographer and videotape producer for catalog, trail crews, photographer, writer, and interpretive guide to lead tours.

"We have had the opportunity to associate with an extraordinary variety of great people." Volunteer from Texas

Wyoming - Bridger-Teton National Forest

Address: Kemmerer Ranger District, Box 31, Kemmerer, WY 83101
Phone: 307-877-4415
Contact: Jerry Rustad/Diane Le Vasseur

Few people visit this fascinating region. There are elk, moose, deer, bear, coyotes, golden eagles, sandhill cranes, and more living in the 300,000 acres of Bridger-Teton National Forest between Jackson Hole, Wyoming, and the Wasatch Mountains of Utah, with more than 250 miles of hiking trails. The scenery ranges from aspen and conifer forests to rolling grass plains with sagebrush as well as many beautiful lakes.

About two miles from Hobble Creek Campground, at 7,400 feet, is Lake Alice, which is about three miles long and over 200 feet deep. It was formed less than 6,000 years ago when a massive landslide occurred creating a large dam over a mile in length. The water from Hobble Creek was stopped and created the lake. You can hike, horseback ride, or mountain bike to the lake. No motorized vehicles are permitted.

Volunteers are welcome as backcountry rangers at Lake Alice to maintain trails, take water samples, talk to users and keep a journal, and possibly work with horses.

Campground hosts are required at three isolated campgrounds—Allred Flat, Hams Fork, and Hobble Creek—to answer questions, provide information, clean the campground, compile use records, do minor maintenance, and collect fees.

Cost:
   FREE.
Number of programs:
   Few.
Age range:
   Over 18.
Children:
   No.
Major emphasis:
   Service projects.
Sample programs:
   Backcountry Ranger, 5 days a week, July 1 to Labor Day, $16 a day. ***Campground Hosts***, 5 days a week, May to October season, $16 a day.
Provides:
   Campsites. Bring tent and camping gear. Water but no electricity available.

Wyoming - Bureau of Land Management

Address: Rawlins District/Lander Resource Area,
PO Box 670, Rawlins, WY 82301
Phone: 307-324-7171
Contact: Ray Hanson

The Bureau of Land Management, responsible for campgrounds and wilderness in this area in Wyoming, needs Campground Hosts for several campgrounds. Two of them are in South Pass Historical Mining Area, which has numerous historic sites, trout fishing and views of the Wind River Mountains.

Assistance is also needed at Cottonwood Campground on Green Mountain, and at Bennett Peak Campground along the North Platte River, with access to the Snowy Mountain Range.

Cost:
FREE.
Number of programs:
Several
Age range:
Over 18.
Children:
No.
Major emphasis:
Service projects.
Sample programs:
Campground Hosts, May 26 to September 4.
Provides:
Campsites. Stipend is negotiable.

ALSO:
BLM/Worland District covers the Big Horn Basin in north central Wyoming and needs people with spelunking skills for work in caves, as well as campground hosts and help on trail maintenance and recreation planning.
Contact:
BLM/Worland District,
PO Box 119, Worland WY 82410
Phone: 307-347-9871
Contact: Dave Atkins

Yellowstone Institute

Address: PO Box 117, Yellowstone National Park, WY 82190
Phone: 307-344-2294:
Fax: 307-344-2294
Contact: Don Nelson

Cost:
$25 to $825. Non-profit organization.

Number of programs:
More than 80.

Age range:
18 and older.

Children:
Some children's courses, minimum age 6.

Major emphasis:
Natural history education in Yellowstone National Park.

Sample programs:
Hiking & Camping in Grizzly Country, 2 days, $85. *Bears: Folklore & Biology*, 3 days, $145. *Family Horsepacking Teton West Slope*, 4 days, $420. *Exploring Yellowstone in Winter*, 9 days, $825.

Provides:
Instruction only for courses at Institute, tuition, meals, and lodging on excursions.

Explore Yellowstone National Park with this year-round educational field program center. Join outdoor courses led by experts in the region on such topics as astronomy, birds, wildflowers, flyfishing, bears, wildlife photography, field journals, natural history, and programs by Native Americans about the Park's role in Indian life. Wilderness horsepacking trips ride through different areas of the park, including the Teton West Slope, Indian routes, fur trapper routes, and the Washburn Expedition trail. Most courses require some walking at higher elevations so participants should be in good health.

For children, there are one-day Nature Detective Workshops on plants, butterflies, geysers, beetles, birds and other topics. For families and children, there are hikes off the beaten track with two former National Park Service rangers and their young sons.

Summer classes meet at the historic Buffalo Ranch in the northeast region of the park. There are heated log cabins available ($8 per person per night), and a central kitchen, bath and classroom building. Campgrounds, commercial cabins and motels are a few miles away. Some courses are offered at Mammoth, where you can stay at the historic Mammoth Hotel, or at a campground. Two winter courses are held in the unusual setting of Canyon Village, with meals served in yurts, rigid portable shelters used by nomadic people.

The Institute, which began in 1974, is sponsored by the Yellowstone Association, a non-profit group founded in 1933 to support educational, historical, and scientific programs for the benefit of the park and its visitors in cooperation with the National Park Service.

Zoetic Research & Sea Quest Expeditions

Address: PO Box 2424, Friday Harbor, WA 98250
Phone: 206-378-5767
Contact: Mark Lewis, Director

This company offers sea kayak trips to explore the Sea of Cortez in Baja, and the San Juan Islands near Washington. Both areas are prime whale-watching centers, and promise exciting glimpses of these huge mammals.

Every trip is led by an experienced kayaker who is a biologist, and who shares his or her comprehensive knowledge of natural history. All groups are limited to 12 participants. No previous kayaking experience is necessary, but you should be in good physical condition.

The company uses extremely stable fiberglass kayaks that hold two paddlers and gear. You paddle for about four hours a day, and then camp out along the shore. If you can hike, bike or swim, you can paddle a kayak. At night, you camp on beaches, eat fresh-cooked meals including fish, salads, vegetables and fruit, and enjoy hiking, snorkeling, and fishing.

Cost:
$49 to $699. Non-profit organization.

Number of programs:
Several.

Age range:
All ages.

Children:
One-day trips, over 5. Other trips, over 12.

Major emphasis:
Marine ecology.

Sample programs:
Whalewatching, one day, $49.00.
Kayaking in Baja California, 5 days, $599.00; 7 days, $699.00.

Provides:
Accommodations, transportation, some meals, guides, instruction, entry fees, equipment, pre-trip orientation, insurance liability.

"Paddling with the whales was the climax of an entirely great trip. The guides made it seem like we were on a scientific expedition!" Participant from Utah

"Outstanding. The trip went beyond my wildest expectations. The guide was extremely knowledgeable and conveyed his enthusiasm to the group." Participant from Washington

APPENDIX

Recommended Travel Guides

Environmental Vacations: Volunteer Projects to Save the Planet. Stephanie Ocko. John Muir Publications, Santa Fe NM 87504.

Family Travel: Terrific New Vacations for Today's Families. Evelyn Kaye. Blue Penguin Publications, Boulder, Colorado.

Farm, Ranch & Country Vacations. Pat Dickerman. Scottsdale AZ 85250.

Going Places: The Guide to Travel Guides. Greg Hayes & Joan Wright. Harvard Common Press, Boston MA.

Helping Out in the Outdoors: A Directory of Volunteer Jobs & Internships in Parks and Forests. Editor: Shirley J. Hearn. American Hiking Society, Washington DC 20041-2160.

International Workcamp Directory. FREE. Volunteers for Peace, Belmont VT 05730.

Maiden Voyages: Writings of Women Travelers. Editor: Mary Morris. Vintage Books/Random House, New York NY.

National Park Guide. Michael Frome. Prentice Hall, Englewood Cliffs, NJ.

Specialty Travel Index: Directory of Special Interest Travel. Editor: Risa Weinrib. Published twice a year. Alpine Hansen Publishers, San Anselmo CA 94960.

Transitions Abroad: The Guide to Learning, Living and Working Overseas. Bi-monthly publication. Amherst, Massachusetts.

Travel and Learn: Where to Go for Everything You'd Love to Know. Evelyn Kaye. Blue Penguin Publications.

Volunteer! The Comprehensive Guide to Voluntary Service in the US and Abroad (1995). Council on International Educational Exchange, New York, New York.

Volunteer Vacations. Bill McMillon. Chicago Review Press, Chicago, IL.

Work your Way Round the World. Susan Griffith. Writers Digest Books, Cincinnati, OH.

Children under 16 Welcome

Adventure Bound
    River Expeditions
Alaska River Journeys
Alaska Wildland Adventures
Arizona Raft Adventures
AWE! American
    Wilderness Experience
Backroads
Canoe Country Escapes
Canyonlands Field Institute
Caretta Turtle Research Project
Colorado Dude
    & Guest Ranch Association
Colorado State Parks Volunteers
Colorado Trail Foundation
Country Inns Along the Trail
Craftsbury Running Camps
Crater of Diamonds State Park
Crow Canyon
    Archaeological Center
Desert Survivors
Dinamation International Society
Dirt Camp for Mountain Bikers
Florida State Parks
Glacier Institute
Gold Vacations - Colorado
Gold Vacations - Georgia
Hostelling International/
    American Youth Hostels
International Wolf Center
Michigan Passport in Time
Montana Passport in Time
Mountain Travel-Sobek

National Audubon Society
National Wildlife Federation
Natural Habitat
Nature Expeditions International
New Mexico Passport in Time
North Cascades Institute
Olympic Park Institute
Oregon Passport in Time
Pacific Catalyst
Paragon Guides
Passport in Time
Pocono Environmental
    Education Center
Roads Less Traveled
Rocky Mountain
    Nature Association
Saga Holidays
Sierra Club Service Trips
Smithsonian Study Tours
Sundance Expeditions
    & Kayak School
Timberline Bicycle Tours
Utah Passport in Time
Vermont State Parks
Victor Emanuel Nature Tours
Virginia Department of
    Conservation & Recreation
Volunteers for Outdoor Colorado
Windjammer Cruises
    Victory Chimes
Yellowstone Institute
Zoetic Research
    & Sea Quest Expeditions

Free Vacations

Alaska State Parks
American Hiking Society
Appalachian Mountain Club
Arizona Navajo
    National Monument
Arizona Passport in Time
Arkansas Hot Springs
    National Park
Arkansas Ouachita
    National Forest
California Department of
    Parks & Recreation
California Lake Tahoe Basin
California Passport in Time
California Sequoia & Kings
    Canyon National Parks
Colorado Mesa Verde
    National Park
Colorado Pike
    & San Isabel National Forests
Colorado State Parks Volunteers
Colorado Trail Foundation
Desert Survivors
Florida Everglades National Park
Florida State Parks
Hawaii Haleakala National Park
Idaho Panhandle National Forest
Idaho-Passport in Time
Indiana Wayne National Forest
Michigan Isle Royale
    National Park
Michigan Passport in Time
Minnesota Voyageurs

    National Park
Montana Little Bighorn
    Battlefield
Montana Passport in Time
New Mexico Carlsbad Caverns
    National Park
New Mexico Passport in Time
North Carolina Blue Ridge
    Parkway
Ohio Department of Natural
    Resources
Oregon Bureau of Land
    Management
Oregon Deschutes
    National Forest
Oregon Passport in Time
Passport in Time
Pennsylvania State Parks
Potomac Appalachian Trail Club
Student Conservation
    Association
Texas Aransas National
    Wildlife Refuge
Utah Bureau of Land
    Management
Utah Canyonlands National Park
Utah Passport in Time
Vermont State Parks
Virginia Department of
    Conservation & Recreation
Virginia George Washington
    National Forest
Volunteers for Outdoor

    Colorado
Volunteers for Outdoor
    Washington
Wisconsin Apostle Islands National
    Lakeshore
Wisconsin Department of Natural
    Resources
Wyoming Bridger/Teton National
    Forest
Wyoming Bureau of Land
    Management

Hiking and Biking Vacations

Adirondack Mountain Club
Alaska Chugach National Forest
Alaska State Parks
Alaska Wildland Adventures
American Hiking Society
Appalachian Mountain Club
Arizona Navajo
    National Monument
Arkansas Hot Springs
    National Park
Arkansas Ouachita
    National Forest
AWE! American Wilderness
    Experience
Backroads
California Department of
    Parks & Recreation
California Lake Tahoe Basin
California Sequoia & Kings
    Canyon National Parks
Colorado Dude & Guest Ranch
    Association
Colorado Pike & San Isabel
    National Forests
Colorado State Parks Volunteers
Colorado Trail Foundation
Country Inns Along the Trail
Country Walkers
Desert Survivors
Dirt Camp for Mountain Bikers
Earthwatch
Florida Everglades National Park
Florida State Parks

Glacier Institute
Hawaii Haleakala National Park
Hostelling International/
    American Youth Hostels
Idaho Panhandle National Forest
Indiana Wayne National Forest
Michigan Isle Royale
    National Park
Minnesota Voyageurs
    National Park
Mountain Travel-Sobek
North Cascades Institute
Olympic Park Institute
Oregon Bureau of Land
    Management
Oregon Deschutes National Forest
Pennsylvania State Parks
Pocono Environmental
    Education Center
Potomac Appalachian Trail Club
Roads Less Traveled
Rocky Mountain
    Nature Association
Sierra Club Service Trips
Smithsonian Study Tours
Student Conservation Association
Texas Aransas
    National Wildlife Refuge
Timberline Bicycle Tours
Utah Bureau of Land Management
Utah Canyonlands National Park
Vermont State Parks

Victor Emanuel Nature Tours
Virginia Department of
    Conservation & Recreation
Virginia George Washington
    National Forest
Volunteers for Outdoor Colorado
Volunteers for Outdoor
    Washington
Wisconsin Apostle Islands
    National Lakeshore
Wisconsin Department of Natural
    Resources
Wyoming Bridger/Teton National
    Forest
Wyoming Bureau of Land
    Management
Yellowstone Institute
Zoetic Research &
    Sea Quest Expeditions

History and Archaeological Vacations

Arizona Navajo National
    Monument
Arizona Passport in Time
Arkansas Hot Springs
    National Park
California Passport in Time
Canyonlands Field Institute
Colorado Mesa Verde
    National Park
Crater of Diamonds State Park
Crow Canyon Archaeological
    Center
Desert Survivors
Dinamation International Society
Earthwatch
Florida State Parks
Gold Vacations - Colorado
Gold Vacations - Georgia
Hawaii Haleakala National Park
Idaho-Passport in Time
International Wolf Center
Michigan Isle Royale
    National Park
Michigan Passport in Time
Montana Little Bighorn Battlefield
Montana Passport in Time
New Mexico Carlsbad Caverns
    National Park
New Mexico Passport in Time
North Cascades Institute
Olympic Park Institute

Oregon Passport in Time
Pacific Catalyst
Passport in Time
Rocky Mountain Nature
    Association
Smithsonian Study Tours
Utah Canyonlands National Park
Utah Passport in Time
Virginia George Washington
    National Forest
Windjammer Cruises
    Victory Chimes
Wisconsin Apostle Islands
    National Lakeshore
Yellowstone Institute

Nature and Wildlife Vacations

Alaska Chugach National Forest
Alaska River Journeys
Alaska Wildland Adventures
AWE! American Wilderness
    Experience
California Lake Tahoe Basin
California Sequoia & Kings
    Canyon National Parks
Canoe Country Escapes
Canyonlands Field Institute
Caretta Turtle Research Project
Colorado Dude & Guest
    Ranch Association
Colorado Pike &
    San Isabel National Forests
Earthwatch
Florida Everglades National Park
Florida State Parks
International Wolf Center
Massachusetts Audubon Society
Mountain Travel-Sobek
National Audubon Society
National Wildlife Federation
Natural Habitat
Nature Expeditions International
North Cascades Institute
Olympic Park Institute
Oregon Deschutes National Forest
Pacific Catalyst
Pocono Environmental
    Education Center
Rocky Mountain Nature
    Association

Texas Aransas National
    Wildlife Refuge
Victor Emanuel Nature Tours
Yellowstone Institute
Zoetic Research & Sea
    Quest Expeditions

Waterways Vacations

Adventure Bound River
  Expeditions
Alaska River Journeys
Alaska Wildland Adventures
Arizona Raft Adventures
Arkansas Hot Springs
  National Park
AWE! American Wilderness
  Experience
California Lake Tahoe Basin
Canoe Country Escapes
Caretta Turtle Research Project
Earthwatch
Florida Everglades National Park
Florida State Parks
Michigan Isle Royale
  National Park
Minnesota Voyageurs
  National Park
Mountain Travel-Sobek
National Audubon Society
National Wildlife Federation
Natural Habitat
Nature Expeditions International
North Cascades Institute
Olympic Park Institute
Oregon Deschutes National Forest
Pacific Catalyst
Sierra Club Service Trips
Smithsonian Study Tours
Student Conservation Association
Sundance Expeditions & Kayak
  School

Texas Aransas National
  Wildlife Refuge
University Research Expeditions
  Program
Victor Emanuel Nature Tours
Virginia Department of
  Conservation & Recreation
Volunteers for Outdoor
  Washington
Windjammer Cruises
  Victory Chimes
Wisconsin Apostle Islands
  National Lakeshore
Zoetic Research & Sea
  Quest Expeditions

National Park Service Regional Offices

Alaska Region
National Park Service
2525 Gambell Street
Anchorage AK 99503-2892

Mid-Atlantic Region
National Park Service
143 South Third Street
Philadelphia PA 19106-2818

Midwest Region
National Park Service
1709 Jackson Street
Omaha NE 68102-2571

National Capital Region
National Park Service
1100 Ohio Drive SW
Washington DC 20242-0001

North Atlantic Region
National Park Service
15 State Street
Boston MA 02109-3572

Pacific Northwest Region
National Park Service
909 First Avenue
Seattle WA 98104-1060

Rocky Mountain Region
National Park Service
PO Box 25287
Denver Co 80225-0287

Southeast Region
National Park Service
75 Spring Street SW
Atlanta GA 30303-3378

Southwest Region
National Park Service
PO Box 728
Santa Fe NM 87504-0728

Western Region
National Park Service
600 Harrison Street, Suite 600
San Francisco CA 94107-1372

US Fish & Wildlife Service Volunteers

Volunteer Coordinator
US Fish & Wildlife Service
PO Box 1306
Albuquerque NM 87103

Volunteer Coordinator
US Fish & Wildlife Service
Richard Russell Federal Bldg
75 Spring St S.W.
Atlanta GA 30303

Volunteer Coordinator
US Fish & Wildlife Service
1011 E Tudor Rd
Anchorage AK 99503

Volunteer Coordinator
US Fish & Wildlife Service
Denver Federal Center
PO Box 25486
Denver CO 80225

Volunteers Director
US Fish & Wildlife Service
One Gateway Center/Suite 700
Newton Corner MA 02158

Volunteer Coordinator
US Fish & Wildlife Service
Federal Bldg, Fort Snelling
Twin Cities MN 55111

Bureau of Land Management Volunteers

For information, write to:
Volunteer Coordinator
BLM State Office
at one of the following addresses:

ALASKA
701 C St
Anchorage AK 99513

ARIZONA
PO Box 16563
Phoenix AZ 85011

CALIFORNIA
2800 Cottage Way
Sacramento CA 95825

COLORADO
2850 Youngfield Street
Lakewood CO 80215

EASTERN STATES
BLM Eastern States
350 S Pickett Street
Alexandria VA 22304

IDAHO
3380 Americana Terrace
Boise ID 83706

MONTANA
222 N 32nd Street
Billings MT 59107

NEVADA
300 Booth Street
Reno NV 89520

NEW MEXICO
PO Box 1449
Santa Fe NM 87501

OREGON
825 NE Multnomah Street
Portland OR 97208

UTAH
324 S State Street
Salt Lake City UT 84111

WYOMING
2515 Warren Avenue
Cheyenne WY 82003

WESTERN STATES
US Forest Pacific NW Region
PO Box 3623
Portland OR 97208

Learning the Lingo

Forest Service Acronyms

AD	Administratively Determined
ARPA	Archaeological Resources Protection Act
AWOL	Absent Without Official Leave
AUM	Animal Unit Month
BD	Brush Disposal
BLM	Bureau of Land Management
BEMA	Bald Eagle Management Area
CFR	Code of Federal Regulations
CO	Contracting Officer
CPU	Central Processing Unit
CRR	Cultural Resource Report
CWN	Call When Needed (Work Status)
DEQ	Department of Environmental Quality
DMT	District Management Team
DR	District Ranger
EA	Environmental Assessment
EDR	Employee Development Record
EE	Environmental Education
EIS	Environmental Impact Statement
EPA	Environmental Protection Agency
FLIPS	Forest Level Information Processing System
FMO	Fire Management Officer
FONSI	Finding Of No Significant Impact
FRC	Federal Records Center
FSH	Forest Service Handbook
FSM	Forest Service Manual
FSS	Federal Supply Schedule
FWP	Federal Womens' Program
FWS	Fish and Wildlife Service

GAO	General Accounting Offfice
GPO	Government Printing Office
GSA	General Services Administration
HCA	Habitat Conservatio Area
ICS	Incident Command System
IDT	Interdisciplinary Team
ITM	Individual Tree Marked
LMP	Land Management Plan
LS	Logging Systems
LTM	Leave Tree Marked
LUP	Land Use Plan
LWA	Land, Water, Air
LWOP	Leave Without Pay
MBF	Thousand Board Feet
NEPA	National Environmental Policy Act (1969)
NFMA	National Forest Management Act (1976)
NFPA	National Forest Products Association
NFPC	National Forestry Program Committee
NLMA	National Lumber Manufacturers Association
OIG	Office of Inspector General
OPM	Office of Personnel Management
OWCP	Office of Workers Compensation Programs
P&M	Protection & Maintenance
PAOT	Persons At One Time
PCNST	Pacific Crest National Scenic Trail
PD	Position Description
PFT	Permanent Full Time
PPT	Permanent Part Time
RA	Resource Assistant
RA	Roadless Area
RARE	Roadless Area Reveiw and Evaluation
RD	Ranger District
RIF	Reduction in Force
RIM	Recreation Information Management
RNA	Research Natural Area
ROS	Recreation Opportunity Spectrum
RPA	Resources Planning Act (1974)
SAF	Society of American Foresters
SF-171	Standard Form Employment Application
SOCO	Supervisor's Office Coordinating Organization
SPC	Stand Improvement Precommercial Thinning
STARS	Sales Tracking and Reporting System
TM	Timber Management
TRI	Total Resource Inventory
TSO	Timber Systems Operations
USDA	United States Department of Agriculture
USDI	United States Department of Interior

182 FREE VACATIONS & BARGAIN ADVENTURES IN THE USA

USFS	United States Forest service
USGS	United States Geological Survey
VA	Veterans Administration
WO	Washington Office
YACC	Young Adult Conservation Corps
YCC	Youth Conservation Corps (Act of 1970)

Park Service Acronyms

IHS	International Historic Site
NB	National Battlefield
NBP	National Battlefield Park
NBS	National Battlefield Site
NHP	National Historical Park
NHS	National Historical Site
NL	National Lakeshore
NM	National Mountain
NMP	National Military Park
N MEM	National Memorial
NP	National Park
NPS	National Park Service
NP & PRES	National Park and Preserve
N PRES	National Preserve
NR	National River
NRA	National Recreational Area
NRR	National Recreational River
N RES	National Reserve
NS	National Seashore
NSR	National Scenic River
NST	National Scenic Trail
WR	Wild River
WSR	Wild and Scenic River

State Tourist Bureaus

Alabama Bureau of Tourism
532 South Perry Street
Montgomery AL 36130
(205)261-4169:/(800)392-8096

Alaska Division of Tourism
Box E
Juneau AK 99811
(907)465-2010

Arizona Tourism Office
1480 E. Bethany Home Road
Phoenix AZ 85014
(602)255-3618

Arkansas Department of Parks
One Capitol Mall
Little Rock AR 72201
(501)682-7777/(800)643-8383

California Tourism Office
1121 L Street
Sacramento CA 95814
(916)322-2882/(800)TO-CALIF

Colorado: Denver Visitor Bureau
225 West Colfax
Denver CO 80202
Phone: (303)892-1505/
 (800)645-3446

Connecticut Dept of Tourism
210 Washington St., Room 900
Hartford CT 06106
(203)566-3948/(800)243-1685

DC Visitors Association
1575 I St NW, Suite 250
Washington DC 20005
(202)787-7000

Delaware Tourism Office
99 Kings Highway,
Box 1401
Dover DE 19903
(302)736-4271/(800)441-8846

Florida Division of Tourism
126 Van Buren Street
Tallahassee FL 32301
(904)487-1462

Georgia Department of Tourism
Box 1776
Atlanta GA 30301
(404)656-3590

Hawaii Visitors Bureau
2270 Kala Kaua Avenue
Honolulu HI 96800
(808)923-1811

Idaho Travel Council
State Capitol Building
Boise ID 83720
(208)334-2470/(800)635-7820

Illinois Travel Center
Department of Commerce
310 S. Michigan Avenue, #108
Chicago IL 60604
(312)793-2094/(800)223-0121

Indiana Tourist Development
1 North Capitol Street
Indianapolis IN 46204
(317)232-8860/
(800)2-WANDER

Iowa Tourist Travel
600 East Court Avenue
Des Moines IA 50309
(515)281-3100/(800)345-IOWA

Kansas Department of Travel
400 West 8th Street/5th floor
Topeka KS 66603
(914)296-2009

Kentucky Department of Travel
2200 Capitol Plaza Tower
Frankfort KY 40601
(502)564-4930/(800)225-TRIP

Louisiana Office of Tourism
Box 94291
Baton Rouge LA 70804
(504)925-3860/(800)334-8626

Maine Division of Tourism
97 Winthrop Street
Hallowell ME 04347
(207)289-2423/(800)533-9595

Maryland Office of Tourism
45 Calvert Street
Annapolis MD 21401
(301)974-3519/(800)331-1750

Massachusetts Tourism
100 Cambridge Street
Boston MA 02202
(617)727-3201/(800)942-MASS

Michigan Travel Bureau
Box 30226
Lansing MI 48909
(517)373-0670/(800)543-2YES

Minnesota Office of Tourism
250 Skyway Level
375 Jackson Street
St. Paul MN 55101
(612)296-5029/(800)328-1461

Mississippi Division of Tourism
1301 Walter Sillers Building
Box 849
Jackson MS 39025
(601)359-3426/(800)647-2290

Missouri Division of Tourism
Truman State Office Building
PO Box 1055
Jefferson City MO 65102
(314)751-4133

Montana Travel Division
1424 9th Avenue
Helena MT 59620
(406)444-2654/(800)541-1447

Nebraska Division of Tourism
301 Centennial Mall South
PO Box 94666
Lincoln NE 68509
(402)471-3794/(800)228-4307

Nevada Tourism Commission
State Capitol Complex
Carson City NV 89710
(702)885-3636/
(800)NEVADA8

New Hampshire Vacation Travel
PO Box 856
Concord NH 03301
(603)271-2665

New Jersey Office of Tourism
CN-826
20 West State Street
Trenton NJ 08625
(609)292-2470/(800)JERSEY7

New Mexico Tourism
Joseph Montoya Building
1100 St. Francis Drive
Santa Fe NM 87503
(505)827-0291/(800)545-2040

New York Division of Tourism
One Commerce Plaza
Albany NY 12245
(518)474-4116/(800)CALL-NYS

North Carolina Tourism Division
430 Salisbury Street
Box 25249
Raleigh NC 27611
(919)733-4171/(800)VISIT-NC

North Dakota Tourism
Liberty Memorial Building
Capitol Grounds
Bismarck ND 58505
(701)224-2525/(800)472-2100

Ohio Department of Tourism
Box 1001
Columbus OH 43266
(614)466-8844/(800)BUCKEYE

Oklahoma Tourism Department
505 Will Rogers Building
Oklahoma City OK 73105
(405)521-2406/(800)652-6552

Oregon Division of Tourism
539 Cottage Street NE
Salem OR 97310
(503)378-3451/(800)547-7842

Pennsylvania Travel Department
416 Forum Building
Harrisburg PA 17120
(717)787-5453/(800)VISIT-PA

Rhode Island Tourism
7 Jackson Walkway
Providence RI 02903
(401)277-2601/(800)556-2484

South Carolina Tourism Dept.
Box 71
Columbia SC 29202
(803)734-0122

South Dakota Tourism
Capitol Lake Plaza
711 Wells Avenue
Pierre SD 57501
(605)773-3301/(800)843-8000

Tennessee Tourism Department
Box 23170
Nashville TN 37202
(615)741-2158

Texas Travel Information
Box 5064
Austin TX 78763
(512)462-9191

Utah Travel Council
Council Hall
Capital Hill
Salt Lake City UT 84114
(801)533-5681

Vermont Travel Division
134 State Street
Montpelier VT 05602
(802)828-3236

Virginia Division of Tourism
Suite 500
202 West 9th Street
Richmond VA 23219
(804)786-2951/(800)VIS-ITVA

Washington State Tourism
101 General Admin. Building
Olympia WA 98504
(206)753-5600/(800)544-1800

West Virginia Tourism Office
State Capitol Complex
Charleston WV 25305
(304)348-2286/
(800)CALL-WVA

Wisconsin Division of Tourism
123 West Washington Avenue
PO Box 7606
Madison WI 53707
(608)266-2161/(800)432-TRIP

Wyoming Travel Commission
Frank Norris Travel Center
I-25 & College Drive,
Cheyenne WY 82002-0660
(307)777-7777/(800)225-5996

USA TERRITORIES

American Samoa Government
Office of Tourism
PO Box 1147
Pago AS 96799
(684)633-5187

Guam Visitors Bureau
Pale San Vitores Road
PO Box 3520
Agana GU 96910
Phone: (671)646-5278

Marianas Visitors Bureau
PO Box 861
Saipan, CM,
Mariana Islands 96950
(670)234-8327

Puerto Rico Tourism Company
PO Box 125268
Miami FL 33102-5268
(212)541-6630/(800)223-6530

US Virgin Islands
Division of Tourism
Box 6400, Vitia
Charlotte Amalie,
St. Thomas, USVI 00801
(809)774-8784/(800)372-8784

Travel Ethic for Environmentally Responsible Tourism

National Audubon Society

The effectiveness of these guidelines rests on the performance and cooperation of the tour operator, naturalist leaders, and expedition travelers. Each of these parties must possess and promote a sense of propriety if the collective effort is to succeed. Harmless viewing of wildlife and habitats in which wildlife abounds can proliferate while preserving both the activity and the resource.

Tourism is one of the fastest growing industries in the world today. In some countries, so far little-known to travelers, where there are huge problems of unemployment and weak national economies, tourism is being regarded as a new primary industry. It creates employment and often brings in foreign currency to economically marginal areas. Sightseers from more affluent nations are ever searching for new places to explore. The trend seems to be growing away from sun, sea, and sand holidays toward adventure, the outdoors, wildlife watching, and cultural interests.

Close encounters with members of the animal kingdom are at very high interest levels. This coincides with a rapidly developing public awareness of environmental matters. Such a combination of conditions could lead to an influx of excursionists into environmentally sensitive areas which, if not carefully managed, could exert pressure and do possibly irrevocable damage to the natural resources it seeks.

The National Audubon Society realizes that the maintenance of these sensitive resources will ensure the continuation of tourism in such areas. The resource in question is the entire natural world, from coastal Alaska and the high Arctic and Greenland, to the wilderness of Antarctica and all that lies between.

The National Audubon Society has become increasingly aware of both the potential and actual conflict between tourism development and the natural environment. We are completely convinced that more can be done to create a positive balance between the two and to create an atmosphere where commercial operators and environmentalists can interact positively. We recognize that tourism can be a powerful tool favoring environmental conservation --

particularly through enhancement of public awareness of environmentally sensitive areas and their resources and the stimulation of action and mobilization of support to prevent the erosion of such environments.

Toward these goals, the National Audubon Society urges all tour operators promoting exploration in wilderness areas to adopt the guidelines here stated.

GUIDELINES

1. Wildlife and their habitats must not be disturbed.

2. Audubon tourism to natural areas will be sustainable.

3. Waste disposal must have neither environmental nor aesthetic impact.

4. The experience a tourist gains in traveling with Audubon must enrich his or her appreciation of nature, conservation, and the environment.

5. Audubon tours must strengthen the conservation effort and enhance the natural integrity of places visited.

6. Traffic in products that threaten wildlife and plant populations must not occur.

7. The sensibilities of other cultures must be respected.

I. Wildlife and their habitats must not be disturbed.

Fragile habitats must not be stressed. Trails will be followed. Plants will be left to grow. In delicate habitats, vegetation destruction and rock slides can easily be caused by the trampling of too many people. Mosses, lichens, and certain wildflowers and grasses may take as much as 100 years or more to regenerate, and must not be walked upon. It is the obligation of the tour company and the naturalist leaders to promote a "stay on the trail" policy. No responsible tour operator or naturalist should allow the removal or picking of plant specimens or other ground cover. Introduction of exotic plant species must be avoided.

Coral reefs. Coral reefs take anywhere from several years to several decades to regenerate. Therefore, the National Audubon Society insists that all of its tour operators provide the broadest protection possible for this underwater life form. Destruction of any part of any coral reef calls for the greatest censure.

Animals. Animal behavior will not be inhibited. Because many of the most well-subscribed tours are operated during the various animals' breeding season, tour operators and leaders should establish and always maintain at least minimum distance from these animals.

Scientific studies predict that a specific animal behavioral function, such as courtship, nesting, or feeding young, demands a specific amount of energy on the part of the breeding animal. Approaching animals too closely can cause them to expend energy needlessly in a fury of defensive territorial display. This can cause an energy deficit that reduces the animals' productivity in the same way as does a food shortage. If disturbances are caused by visitors early enough in the breeding cycle, the parents may abandon the breeding site. Additionally, while the adults are warding off intruders, eggs and young are vulnerable to chilling, and unguarded young are most susceptible to predation.

Minimum distance. Animals will not be harassed or approached too closely. Our recommendation is that all tour participants keep a minimum distance of 20 to 30 feet from seals, walruses, otters, giant tortoises, lava lizards, sea turtles, koalas, all marsupials, and unwary plains herd animals. We recommend that all visitors stay on the periphery of animal assemblages e.g. penguin colonies, seabird colonies, albatrosses on nests, courting groups, etc. This means:

√   Visitors should never be allowed to surround an animal or group of animals.

√   Visitors and leaders must remain alert never to get between animal parents and their young.

√   Visitors must never be allowed to get between marine mammals and the water's edge.

√   Nesting raptors should be viewed only through binoculars or telescopes at considerable distances from the nest.

√   Crowd control ethics include keeping the decibel level as low as possible, thereby minimizing the potential threat to animals.

√   Touching animals should never be allowed.

Photography. The advent of sophisticated photographic technology means that even amateur photographers can get professional-looking photographs while keeping a respectable distance from the subject. Photography of birds and animals should never include the removal of nestlings or young from the nest, or removal of foliage or camouflage from close to the breeding site. Removals of animals from burrows, dens, caves, or tree cavities must be prohibited at all times.

Relentlessly following or harassing birds or animals for the sake of a photograph should never be allowed. Lingering obtrusively in close proximity to a nesting site, preventing the animal from returning to the site, should never be allowed.

Every effort will be made to minimize a visit's impact, and if that effort is inadequate, the visit will be curtailed.

2. Audubon tourism to natural areas will be sustainable.

Audubon will encourage local guides, landowners, and conservation representatives to develop and implement long-term visitor plans to ensure the sustainable use of their wildlife habitats. Audubon also encourages patronage of locally benign concessionaires.

3. Waste disposal must have neither environmental nor aesthetic impacts.

All tour operators must take into account the fragility of the areas visited with regard to proper waste disposal.

Cruise ships. All cruise ships, whether operating in the Arctic or sub-Arctic, the Great Barrier Reef of Australia, the islands of the Southern Ocean, along the Antarctic Peninsula, the Pacific shores of South America and Galapagos, or along the reaches of the Orinoco and Amazon rivers must commit to a shipboard anti-dumping/anti-garbage policy. This policy ensures that the shipboard crew and staff will not foul any waters, particularly with regard to non-biodegradable (plastic) materials.

If necessary, all trash must be contained and carried back to a port where proper disposal is available. Any tour operator offering the opportunity for visiting land wilderness areas overnight or for several days must make provision for carrying out all trash generated while there. The tour operator and naturalists should promote an attitude of keeping every specific site as clean as possible. No littering of any kind should be tolerated.

The National Audubon Society will neither patronize nor approve any vendor that does not **strictly** adhere to this guideline.

4. The experience a tourist gains in traveling with Audubon must enrich his or her appreciation of nature, conservation, and the environment.

Every trip to a wilderness area must be led by experienced, well-trained, responsible naturalists and guides. These naturalists should have a solid background in the various habitats to be visited, the flora and fauna contained there, and the sensitive nature of those habitats. These naturalists and guides must be able to provide proper supervision of the visitors, prevent disturbances to the area, answer questions of the visitors regarding the flora and fauna of the area, and present the conservation issues relevant to the area.

Group size. All tour operators should provide adequate space for these naturalists so that the leader-to-group size ratio never exceeds one to 25. The maximum size of a visiting group will depend upon the fragility of the surroundings, in which case the ratio could drop to as little as one in ten.

These naturalist-guides serve as the environmental conscience of the group and, as such, should be an integral part of every tour.

5. Audubon Tours must strengthen the conservation effort and enhance the natural integrity of places visited.

One constant theme in Audubon tours will be the problems facing wildlife and their habitat, and the solutions that may be achieved. On tours particularly to other countries, contacts will be sought and established with conservation organization working in the area visited. Their representatives will be encouraged to speak to our tours and sought, when appropriate, to serve as local naturalist leaders and lecturers to accompany Audubon en route.

6. Traffic in products that threaten wildlife and plant populations must not occur.

The National Audubon Society cannot condone a laissez-faire attitude with regard to purchase of certain types of souvenirs or mementoes. Habitat loss remains the single largest threat to animal species. However, commerce and poaching have also depleted countless animal and plant populations.

All our vendors must conscientiously educate their travelers against buying the following items:

√ All sea turtle products, including jewelry, sea turtle eggs skin cream made from turtle meat.

√ Most reptile skins and leathers, particularly those from Latin America, the Caribbean, China, Egypt (including all crocodile products).

√ Snakeskin products from Latin America and Asian countries, including India.

√ Lizardskin products made of pangolin (anteater) from Thailand, Malaysia, and Indonesia.

√ Ivory from any source, especially worked ivory from elephants and marine mammals, such as whales, walruses, and narwhals.

√ Birds, including large parrots from Australia, Brazil, Ecuador, Paraguay, Venezuela, and the Caribbean islands.

√ Wild birds, and their feathers and skins, used in or as artwork, including mounted birds.

√ Coral from the Caribbean, Southeast Asia, Australia.

√ Furs of spotted cats such as snow leopard, jaguar, ocelot.

√ Furs and fur products of seals and other marine mammals and polar bears.

√ Any orchids and cacti.

7. The sensibilities of other cultures must be respected.

Audubon tours travel in areas of widely varying ethics and practices. On our trips we are the guests of these cultures and our opportunities are to learn and enrich our own understanding of human nature, not to intrude and criticize. In the long run, our abilities to advance conservation will be strengthened by the bridges that understanding will establish.

INDEX

acid rain 88, 188
actors 27
Adirondack 69
Alaska 15, 19, 71, 72, 73, 74, 76,77, 83, 117, 123, 124
126, 127, 136, 146, 160
alligators 106, 107
Anasazi 57, 78, 90, 93, 101, 158
Appalachian 77, 130, 141
Arapaho 121
archaeology 25, 27, 79, 86, 87, 101, 114, 115, 122, 129
138, 145, 153, 154
Arizona 59, 76, 78, 79, 80, 83, 98, 103, 117, 127, 142, 146, 155
Arkansas 81, 100, 145
artifacts 27, 79, 119, 122, 153
artists 27, 107, 115, 140
astronomy 166
backpacking 23, 76, 83, 118, 131, 133, 140
bathhouses 81
battlefield 121
bear 19, 71, 106, 108, 120, 123, 126, 127, 164, 166
beaver 120
biking 25, 26, 72, 83, 84,86, 94, 96,97, 99, 104, 127, 142, 150, 164
biologists 26, 94, 106, 113, 115, 120
birds 45, 107, 117, 120, 123, 124, 125, 127, 131, 132
136, 140, 149, 155, 157, 163, 166
blueberries 89, 162
bookstore 47, 48
butterflies 131, 132, 133, 143, 166
California 15, 76, 84, 85, 87, 88, 98, 102, 112, 117
138, 146, 150, 151, 160
canoeing 25, 83, 89, 99, 113, 140
caribou 72, 74, 123
carpenters 25, 27, 149
Catskill Mountains 69, 77
caves 115, 128
Cheyenne 121
Chinese 135

READERS RESPONSE REQUEST

Blue Penguin Publications specializes in travel resource guides that provide information about where to find outstanding and unusual vacations. So far, the topics we have covered are educational and learning vacations, family trips that are affordable and fun for all ages, and free vacations that won't cost you a penny and benefit the environment.

We know that our readers are aware, informed and experienced travelers, who want value, interest, and satisfaction from their vacations. We are considering how to expand our publications in ways that would be most beneficial to our readers. We'd love to hear from you, if you would take a moment to answer our questions.

Comments:

Where did you find this book?

❏Library   ❏Bookstore   ❏Friend   ❏Mail order

Have you heard about these guides before? ❏Yes ❏No

If yes, where? ....

What did you like most about the book?

....

Which vacations are most interesting to you?

....

What did you like least about the book?

....

How would you improve it?

....

List your favorite vacations:

....

Please use the column on left for comments.
Thank you for your time. If you would like to be put on our mailing list, please include:

Name: .... **Phone:** ....

Address: ....

....

Send completed form to:
Blue Penguin Publications
3031 Fifth Street, Boulder CO 80304

MORE BLUE PENGUIN BOOKS by EVELYN KAYE

Free Vacations and Bargain Adventures in the USA

"The single most comprehensive source of information."

The New York Times reviewing Eco-Vacations

Discover real bargains and great vacations! Here's a guide to hundreds of unforgettable free vacations in beautiful state and national parks in the USA, plus affordable adventure vacations where you hike, bike, raft, and run.

Free Vacations is the completely revised and updated second edition of *Eco-Vacations*.

FREE VACATIONS
Author: Evelyn Kaye
Size: 8½ x 11 softcover. 200 p.
Illustrations. Resource lists. Index.
Price: $19.95
ISBN: 0-9626231-7-2
LC:95-060400

Travel and Learn: Where to Go for Everything You'd Love to Know

Award-winning guide in NEW 3rd edition.

More than 1,700 fascinating programs on arts, archaeology, crafts, ecology, language, nature, and outdoor adventure offered by museums, universities, colleges, and organizations, including the Smithsonian, Elderhostel, and Cornell's Adult University.

TRAVEL AND LEARN
Author: Evelyn Kaye
Size: 8½ x 11 softcover. 244 p.
Illustrated. Resource lists. Index.
Price: $19.95
ISBN 0-9626231-5-6
LC 94-070200

Family Travel: Terrific New Vacations for Today's Families

"A nice overview of non-traditional family vacation possibilities."

Family Travel Times

A goldmine of exciting, unusual, and affordable vacation ideas for families of all ages. Discover where you can:

√ hunt for dinosaurs
√ see parrots in a rain forest
√ float lazily in a houseboat
√ stay rent-free in Europe.

FAMILY TRAVEL
Author: Evelyn Kaye
Size: 8½ x 11 softcover. 220 p.
Illustrated. Resource Lists. Index.
Price: $19.95
ISBN 0-9626231-3-X
LC 93-090008

Amazing Traveler: The Biography of a Victorian Adventurer

"A spectacular biography!"

Kitty Kelley, biographer

The inspiring story of Isabella Bird, a 19th century English woman, who despite ill-health became the outstanding explorer and author of her day. She trekked in the mountains of Tibet, walked across Hawaii's volcanoes, traveled through the Far East, and rode a camel across the Sinai desert.

AMAZING TRAVELER:
ISABELLA BIRD
Author: Evelyn Kaye
Size: 5½ x 8½ softcover. 224 p.
Illustrated. Bibliography. Index.
Price: $19.95
ISBN 0-9626231-6-4.
LC 94-94504

ORDER FORM
Call 1-800-800-8147

YES! Please send me:
..... copies of FREE VACATIONS
..... copies of TRAVEL & LEARN
..... copies of FAMILY TRAVEL
..... copies of AMAZING TRAVELER
Each book $19.95 + $2.55 shipping = $22.50
10% discount for 2 or more books
TOTAL enclosed: $ ....

Make check payable to:
BLUE PENGUIN PUBLICATIONS,
3031 Fifth Street, Boulder, CO 80304
303-449-8474 Fax:303-449-7525

MasterCard/Visa # ....
expires . /......
Name ....
Address ....
City .... State .... Zip ....
Phone ....

TOTAL GUARANTEE. Your money back if you are not completely satisfied. No questions asked!